Camping Ohio

Help Us Keep This Guide Up to Date

Every effort has been made by the author and editors to make this guide as accurate and useful as possible. However, many things can change after a guide is published—campgrounds open and close, grow and contract; regulations change; facilities come under new management, and so forth.

We appreciate hearing from you concerning your experiences with this guide and how you feel it could be improved and kept up to date. While we may not be able to respond to all comments and suggestions, we'll take them to heart, and we'll also make certain to share them with the author. Please send your comments and suggestions to the following address:

Globe Pequot Press
Reader Response/Editorial Department
P.O. Box 480
Guilford, CT 06437

Or you may e-mail us at:

editorial@GlobePequot.com

Thanks for your input, and happy camping!

Camping Ohio

A Comprehensive Guide to Public Tent and RV Campgrounds

Bob Frye

FALCONGUIDES

GUILFORD, CONNECTICUT
HELENA, MONTANA
AN IMPRINT OF GLOBE PEQUOT PRESS

FALCONGUIDES®

FalconGuides is an imprint of Globe Pequot Press.
Falcon, FalconGuides, and Outfit Your Mind are registered trademarks of Morris Book Publishing, LLC.

All interior photos by Bob Frye unless noted otherwise.

Maps: Melissa Baker © Morris Book Publishing, LLC.
Project editor: David Legere
Layout: Lisa Reneson

ISBN 978-0-7627-8180-5

Printed in the United States of America

10 9 8 7 6 5 4 3 2 1

To Hannah, aka Peggy Sue, my Buckeye State camping buddy

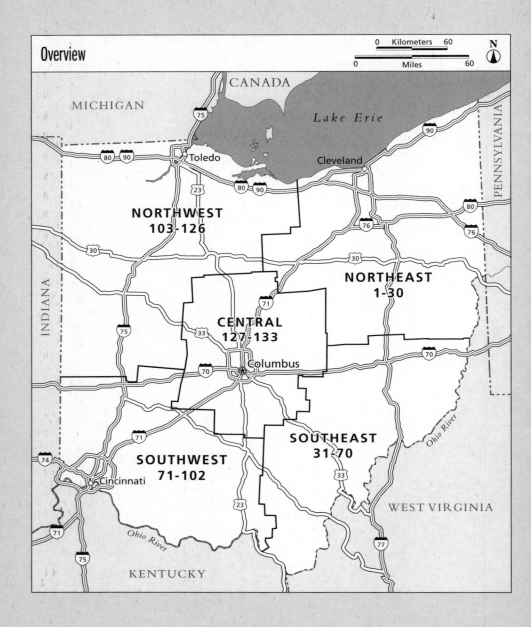

Overview

CANADA

MICHIGAN

Lake Erie

Toledo

Cleveland

NORTHWEST
103-126

PENNSYLVANIA

INDIANA

NORTHEAST
1-30

CENTRAL
127-133

Columbus

SOUTHWEST
71-102

Cincinnati

SOUTHEAST
31-70

Ohio River

WEST VIRGINIA

Ohio River

KENTUCKY

N

Kilometers
Miles

Contents

Acknowledgments

There was a time when Ohio was on the western edge of the frontier. That's true no longer. But there are many, many places still where you can get outside and enjoy nature by hiking, biking, paddling, fishing, hunting, or whatever. And, in what is often the best part, you can turn your adventures into multi-day excursions. Ohio has an abundance of public campgrounds, big and small.

In my experience, all are run by dedicated managers, rangers, maintenance crews, and others. They work hard, often despite shrinking budgets, to keep our outdoors fun, safe, and exciting. A thank you to them all.

And thanks to my wife, Mandy, and sons, Derek and Tyler, who, when they're not with me, keep things rolling along at home. Thank you for picking up the slack.

A solitary lotus stands reflected in the water of one of the bays at Lake Loramie State Park.

Introduction

Ohio is an interesting and varied place.

It's a border state, in a sense, where the edge of the Mid-Atlantic meets the edge of the Midwest. Its topography reflects that. The extreme southeast corner of the state is more like neighboring West Virginia than western Ohio. The former is a land of steep hills and water-cut gorges, wild and rugged feeling. It's there you go to explore the caves and caverns that hid horse thieves and hermits. The latter is farm country, mile upon flat mile of cornfields and silos edged by woodlots. It's a rich land, for the abundant and varied wildlife that thrives there as much as for people.

In between those two zones are reservoirs big and small. The water in many of them is consistently brown and muddy looking, something that's been true since Native Americans roamed here. But they, too, are productive.

And to the north? Northern Ohio, from east to west, fronts Lake Erie, one of the five Great Lakes. That means beaches, surf, and world-class fishing. Where else could you camp on islands big enough to hold not just tents, but also towns with restaurants, shops, bars, and even fire departments?

No matter what section of the state you're talking about, though, there are a lot of people. The state ranks in the top seven nationally in terms of population, with about 11.5 million people. Two of its cities, Columbus and Cleveland, are among the fifty most populous in the nation.

Yet the state ranks just thirty-fourth nationally in terms of square miles. When you factor in how much of Ohio's mass is covered by water, you realize there's a good bit of humanity packed onto the earth within these borders. Wilderness, there's not. Not on any real big scale, anyway.

That said, the state offers some exciting opportunities for those who like to explore the outdoors.

There are many, many lakes across the state, and there are a lot of parks and campgrounds connected to them. Boaters could have a lot of fun traveling from one to another, camping here, then there, waterskiing and tubing, and fishing for walleyes and catfish and muskies along the way. Ohio is a horseman's heaven, too. Many of the parks—federal, state, and local—cater to riders, with designated bridle trails and even campsites crafted specifically with the equine crowd in mind. Off-road and all-terrain vehicle fans will find plenty of trails to use as well.

Those who prefer to enjoy their nature at a slower pace and in quieter environs can also experience good times. Ohio is home to a number of state and federally designated scenic rivers, so paddlers can float through vivid country full of interesting wildlife. Hiking trails are plentiful, with several of the long-distance variety. Birders can see a multitude of species, given the variety of habitat types.

In short, if there's something you want to do outdoors, you can probably find room to do it in Ohio.

Campers can often experience that in the season of their choosing. Most state parks, and many local ones, are open year-round. You may have to do without some amenities if you travel outside the peak season. Some campgrounds close their showers and turn off their water after the first frost. Your choice of sites may be limited too. Many state parks in particular keep just a portion of their campgrounds open after October, and, while they will guarantee you a site if you call to make a reservation, they won't guarantee you a specific site.

But if you're willing to make do and are flexible about where you stay, fun awaits.

Going out in Ohio means you need to keep some safety concerns in mind. The state does see tornadoes, with June, May, July, April, and August, in that order, when they're most likely to hit. Obviously, that's the peak of the camping season, so it pays to know what to do if the weather gets bad.

A group called the Ohio Committee for Severe Weather Awareness encourages people to keep the acronym "DUCK" in mind. It stands for: go Down to the lowest level, get Under something, Cover your head, and Keep in shelter until the storm passes.

State park officials also suggest that campers should discuss with every member of the party what to do if a tornado approaches before one arrives. They also suggest you pay attention to weather forecasts. A tornado watch means conditions are favorable for one to occur; a warning means one has been sighted. Keep an eye on the western sky, as that's where storms will come from. Parks do not have designated storm shelters but you might try a showerhouse of other structure in a pinch. Otherwise, look for any low spot in the landscape that might protect you from flying debris.

It's also critical to pay attention to the weather when on Lake Erie. It's a great place to boat and fish. But it is also a relatively shallow lake, especially in comparison to its width and breadth. Storms can crop up on it suddenly, creating large and dangerous waves in the process. It can go from peaceful and serene to raging and deadly very quickly. If you see or hear about a storm approaching, get off the water.

Keep those things in mind, play it smart, be as wise as you are adventurous, and there are wonderful opportunities to explore the Buckeye State and all it has to offer outdoors. Hopefully, this book helps you explore some of that wonderful country, spending the night here and there while taking in the beauty of its woods, fields, fish, and wildlife. Have fun!

Ohio's Public Campgrounds

This is a comprehensive look at the public campgrounds in Ohio: those run in state parks by the Department of Natural Resources; in Wayne National Forest by the USDA Forest Service; at lakes owned by the US Army Corps of Engineers; those managed by the Muskingum Watershed Conservancy District; and by assorted counties, fairgrounds, townships, and cities. These are the places where you pull in, pay a fee—though not always everywhere—and set up shop either at a designated, numbered site or in an open space where you pick your own spot. Sometimes there will be some creature comforts waiting for you; other times there won't. I tell you what to expect at each campground and what you can look forward to doing while you are there.

I also tell you, if in slightly less detail, about the other options when it comes to camping on public land in Ohio. There's a lot of "dispersed" camping available in the national forest, so we tell you how that works. There are also some designated backpacking areas that offer things like water and bathrooms; we talk about those a bit, too.

In Ohio as elsewhere it's also possible to "camp" under a roof. There are cabins—some well-equipped, others more primitive—that you can rent. There are also cottages, old houses lodges, and more. We describe those opportunities too.

The one thing not covered here is private campgrounds. There are thousands of those spread around Ohio. Many are the kind of place where people set up trailers and leave them year-round; others cater to weekend tent campers and the like. Details on many of them are available from the Ohio Campground Owners Association, which can be reached at (614) 221-7748 or www.ohiocampers.com.

State Parks

Ohio's Department of Natural Resources administers the state park system. Parks are spread all around the state. There are seventy-seven all told, fifty-six of them with campgrounds open to tents and RVs. Some parks are big, covering thousands of acres. Others are just a few hundred acres, though sometimes surrounded by larger state forests or federal land. Many have lakes, most have playgrounds, and some have unique features all their own.

State parks are generally well regarded. www.tripleblaze.com, a website that rates campgrounds, listed the park system's Hocking Hills State Park Campground as the best in the nation in 2012. Two others made the top 100: Indian Lake State Park, at number 45, and Paint Creek State Park at number 47.

Campers can enjoy discounts at times. The park system sometimes offers 25 percent off the price of camping in early fall, after school is in session and before the peak of the fall foliage season. Ohio residents can also get a Golden Buckeye card that

Visitors to Beaver Creek State Park will be wowed by the views offered of its scenic river.

offers 50 percent off the cost of a campsite Sunday through Thursday and 10 percent off on Friday and Saturday. Campers can also earn points; get enough and you can stay in some parks for free. Information is available by calling (866) 644-6727 or visiting www.ohio.reserveworld.com.

Most state park campgrounds are open year-round, but that comes with a qualifier. Some amenities, like water, may not be available in the off-season. Some sites likely won't be available either. Many parks keep only a portion of their campgrounds open in winter. You have to call the park directly to get a reservation and even then it will only guarantee you a site, not a particular one. Chances are you can always find a place to camp, as crowds are rarely if ever an issue. But be aware that the rules are a bit different then.

Throughout the year, the maximum length of stay in state parks is fourteen days. That's the case in most other kinds of parks too, except for where season-long rentals are available.

USDA Forest Service

Ohio is home to one national forest, the Wayne, which covers almost 250,000 acres. It's located in southeastern Ohio and is broken down into units, the Ironton Ranger District, Athens Ranger District, and Athens Ranger District/Marietta Unit. The forest service motto of "Land of Many Uses" applies here, for better and worse. The good is that there's plenty to do if you like to be outside. There's quiet paddling, opportunities to fish and hunt and more. The Wayne's trail system is especially noteworthy. There are more than 300 miles of trail across the forest, open to horseback riding, hiking, biking, and all-terrain and off-road vehicle riding.

There are two scenic byways across the forest, too, and several historic sites. Be sure to visit Tinker's Cave, an impressive rock shelter used by a reputed horse thief who used the area as his base of operations. The Payne Cemetery, a spot on the Underground Railroad, is worth seeing, too, as are the Shawnee and Snake Ridge lookout towers.

US Army Corps of Engineers

The Army Corps is divided into multiple segments in Ohio. All serve the same primary purpose, to manage locks and dams on the state's rivers and to offer flood control via its impoundments. Providing recreation is a secondary part of its mission. That said, Corps impoundments offer plenty for those who love the outdoors.

At two lakes that straddle the Ohio-Pennsylvania border, the Corps operates campgrounds on its own. Shenango and Berlin Lake are run by the Pittsburgh District of the Corps in Pennsylvania. Elsewhere across Ohio, the campgrounds at Corps lands are run through cooperative agreements with other public agencies, usually either the Department of Natural Resources or Muskingum River Watershed Conservancy.

In all cases, water-based activities are the draw at Corps facilities. Many surround large bodies of water where boaters can operate without horsepower restrictions and enjoy activities like powerboating, tubing, waterskiing, and the like.

Muskingum Watershed Conservancy District

The Conservancy District is a political entity that's been around since 1933. Its official role is to limit flooding and conserve water for public use across more than 8,000 square miles in all or parts of eighteen counties. Check the conservancy's mission statement, though, and you'll see it's big on providing recreation too. To do that, it manages campgrounds and a host of other facilities on five parks. It also runs campgrounds at two marinas. All of its facilities are large and diverse.

Counties and Fairgrounds

Ohio is divided into eighty-eight counties and a surprising number of them offer public camping. Generally, county parks—with a couple of notable exceptions—are smaller in overall size. Their campgrounds are correspondingly smaller and sometimes capable of handling only tents or shorter RVs. The camping season can be shorter too.

But several of these campgrounds are located where other public options are limited, which alone makes them valuable.

Where there are no county parks, another option is county fairgrounds. Quite a few allow camping. Some actively recruit campers; others take them as they come, with their "campground" clearly secondary to the fair's other priorities. Always, you have to work around the county fair when vendors, farmers, and the like get priority or even sole use of the grounds. But these can be good, less-crowded options.

Campground Entries

This book divides the state's campgrounds up into five regions: northeast, southeast, southwest, northwest, and central.

For purposes of organizing state parks—which account for about half of all the public campgrounds in the state—the Department of Natural Resources divides Ohio the same way. You can see the listing at www.dnr.state.oh.us/facilitiesmaps/ohiocamping/tabid/497/Default.aspx.

Maps within the book give you an at-a-glance-look at the campgrounds in each region. Charts detail the amenities and recreational opportunities they offer. There's also a short but specific overview of each region outlining its history, geography, and attractions.

Each campground also gets its own listing, including the following details:

Location: This is the nearest town that shows up on a map so that you can get your general bearings.

Season: This is the period when the campground is open. There are a couple of things to keep in mind.

First, while all of the parks mentioned in this book are open to visitors year-round, many of the campgrounds within them are two- or three-season operations. And within that window, facilities can sometimes vary. For example, a campground that offers flush toilets and showers in mid-summer may operate only vault toilets in fall. It's always best to call the campground to be sure.

Second, some campgrounds stay open later into the year than others specifically to cater to hunters looking to get out for Ohio's gun deer season. That's not to say only hunters can camp; anyone can. But about half a million people hunt deer in Ohio each fall. Hit campgrounds around areas open to hunting then and you can expect deer-hunting neighbors in many places in late November and early December.

Third, campgrounds periodically close for maintenance or other reasons, so always check in advance to be sure a campground will be open when you get there.

Sites: This tells you the total number of campsites available and a little bit about them. Some, for example, are walk-in only, while others may have electric or be ADA accessible.

Maximum RV length: How big of an RV can the campground accommodate? You'll find that here. Size restrictions, when there are any, vary by facility.

Be aware that not all of the pads within a campground are equally long. A campground that says it can accommodate 75-foot RVs may have just one site that big, with the rest 50 feet or shorter. If you've got an especially large rig, call ahead to make sure you can get the space you need.

Facilities: Does the campground have flush toilets and showers or outhouses? Electricity and a sanitary dump station? How about a camp store, a launch for your boat or laundry facilities? This section tells you what facilities are available at each campground.

Fee per night: Prices change constantly, and can even vary within a campground based on whether you're taking a walk-in tent site, a boat-in site or one with electric service for a 40-foot RV. Because of that, we've used a coded system.

$ = Less than $10

$$ = $10 to $15

$$$ = $16 to $20

$$$$ = More than $20

If the price code for a campground indicates a range (say $-$$$), that means you've got options.

A few parks, as is noted in the individual descriptions, offer cabins, cottages, and even lodges. We note their availability, but be aware that the price codes do not account for them. You'll need to call individual parks or check out the reservation systems for those fees.

People sixty-two years of age or older and disabled veterans can often receive discounts on the base campsite fee at state and national campgrounds. Inquire about the discount through individual park offices.

Pets: Some campgrounds allow leashed pets in all their sites; others limit them to certain sites, and some don't allow them at all.

Activities: Does the campground or surrounding area have hiking or mountain biking trails? A pool or swimming beach? Does it offer environmental education programming or fishing or hunting opportunities? This section tells you what you can do in the campground and the park around it.

Management: This is the agency that owns and/or operates the campground.

Contact: Here you get the website for the park that holds this campground. Those websites often offer details on such things as the park's history, updates on conditions or changes, firewood availability, or restrictions and other advisories, and more. You can sometimes find maps here too. That's especially true of state park websites, which offer maps of the parks and campgrounds, and sometimes hiking or birding trail maps.

This section also offers the phone number for each park and/or campground. You'll note that some of the smallest state parks are all managed from one central office.

Also listed are details on whether campgrounds accept reservations—some do not—and how to make them. When it comes to federal and state campgrounds, you can usually make reservations online or by phone. County park campgrounds usually require that you make a phone call.

Of course, you can take your chances on getting space on a walk-in basis just about anywhere, paying your fees on the honor system. But that can be risky at peak times. If you want to be sure there's a site waiting for you when you arrive at a park, call ahead.

Finding the campground: These are turn-by-turn directions to the campground and/or park from the nearest town that shows up on a map. The office is your best spot to pick up maps, brochures, and other information.

The entrance to Kiser Lake State Park is marked by a rainbow of color, with flowers surrounding the park sign.

By the way, it's probably obvious that our highway abbreviation I stands for Interstate and US for U.S. Highway. Not so obvious is that SR indicates an Ohio State Route and TH stands for a Township Highway.

GPS coordinates: These coordinates were generated using mapping software. In most cases, they will take you to the campground, though in parks with more than one campground they may take you to the main campground or to the park office.

A word of caution here: Because of the remote character of some areas, following a GPS device rather than using a map can take you over narrow, often rough, dirt forest service roads. In some instances these devices have directed users to follow "roads" that are in fact only power line or gas line rights-of-way.

Other: If this campground or park offers cabins or cottages, hosts special events like a craft festival or fair, or contains a theater, you'll find that information here. You'll also be told if the park has an organized group tenting area, in case you want to camp here with scouts or some other group.

About the campground: Here you get a few tips on whether the campground is spacious or a bit cramped, which sites offer the best views or access to hiking or the water, whether sites are shaded or in the sun and more.

Why it's worth a visit: Of all the campgrounds in the state, why make a point of visiting this particular one? That's what you'll learn here.

You can find space to take a walk just about anywhere, but some parks are renowned for their trails and the views they lead to. Many parks offer lakes. Some are open to boats with giant motors that can haul skiers; others are small and perfect for exploring on misty mornings with a canoe or kayak. You can expect to see squirrels and raccoons or at least evidence of them in every park you visit. But some are the gateways to viewing bald eagles.

These descriptions explain what it is that makes each park, and each campground, special. They also tell you when might be the best time to visit.

Camping Ohio Amenities Charts

KEY

Hookups:Y = yes, N= no

Toilets: F = flush,V = vault

Showers:Y = yes, N= no

Drinking water:Y = yes, N= no

Dump station:Y = yes, N= no

Recreation: H = hiking, B = boating, F = fishing, S = swimming, C = cycling,
   L = boat launch, R = horseback riding, EE = environmental education, U = hunting,
   O = off-road vehicle area

Fee: $-$$$$

Reservation:Y = yes, N= no

Other "Camping"

If you've got a tent to pitch or an RV to park, there are public options available to you in Ohio other than its "official" campgrounds. There is what's known as dispersed camping, as well as opportunities to go backpacking. We'll touch on each briefly.

Primitive Camping

If you want to camp alone and are willing to rough it, Wayne National Forest allows what's known as primitive camping. This is a create-your-own-space option. You can pitch a tent or park your RV anywhere within the forest so long as you don't block developed trailheads or road rights-of-way. This type of camping is particularly popular with anglers looking to get right on a trout stream, hunters interested in stomping around a particular valley, and hikers looking to access a particular set of challenges.

There are some rules to follow. Campers need to provide their own water. Forest officials discourage people from filtering water on site because so much of it contains heavy metals, a byproduct of past mining practices across the state. Bring what you'll need. Account for your garbage and waste. Open campfires are permitted except when in rock shelters and anywhere when conditions are very dry. They should always be small and contained, though. Be sure your fire is out before leaving an area. And only use downed and dead wood; do not cut any live shrubs or trees.

Primitive camping is free. You generally do not need to check in with the forest service before picking a campsite, unless you are part of a group of twenty-five or more people. Then you need a permit and prior approval. The maximum length of stay in any one location is fourteen consecutive days. You have to be aware that some forest roads are gravel and dirt and get no winter maintenance, so the spot that's perfect in summer may not be accessible later in the year.

Dispersed camping is not for everyone. But this is a fun option if you're comfortable doing things on your own, don't need a lot in the way of amenities, and like quiet.

Backpacking

Wayne National Forest offers some wonderful backpacking opportunities of two kinds. The first is on official trails. There are some trail systems—like the Symmes Creek/Morgan Sister Trail system—that were designed with backpackers in mind. They do not offer shelters or water or other amenities. But there are mapped, blazed trails you can follow on your way in and out of the woods. The second is do-it-yourself backpacking. Forest rules say backpackers can wander anywhere they want, stopping when and where they want, without having to check in or secure a permit.

In both cases there are some things you should keep in mind. In fall, when hunting seasons are in full swing, wear bright orange clothing just like hunters do so that

Campers looking to stay in something other than a tent or RV can check out the cabins offered in various locations around the state, such as these at Lake Hope State Park.

you're visible. Remember that the national forest and its assorted pieces are not always continuous. They exist as patchworks on the landscape, intermingled with parcels of private property. Be aware of where you are and respect private lands. Keep away from oil and gas operations, even on public land. The equipment is privately owned and potentially dangerous.

Ohio's state forests and parks also allow for some backpacking, as do a couple of county parks. As a general rule, those opportunities are slightly more restrictive in nature. Backpackers can camp only at designated sites. Self-registration permits are often required. Fires are prohibited except where fire rings are already in place and you can't stay more than one night at any location.

But there's some fun exploring to do. The 23-mile Zaleski State Forest Back-packing Trail is a very nice one, as is the 60-mile Shawnee State Forest Backpacking Trail. The latter even offers opportunities—with prior approval and a permit—to camp in the forest's 8,000-acre wilderness area. Mohican Memorial State Forest has some park-and-pack camping—described later in this book—that can serve as novice backpacking sites. State parks with backpacking include Burr Oak, Caesar Creek, Tar Hollow, and East Fork. Don't overlook the backpacking trail offered by Five Rivers MetroParks either.

And if you really want to rack up the miles, consider hiking the Buckeye Trail or the North Country Trail. The Buckeye is a roughly 1,400-mile trail that circles

Ohio. It's broken down into twenty-six sections. Information is available at www .buckeyetrail.org. The North Country Trail is a America's longest National Scenic Trail, stretching 4,600 miles from New York to North Dakota. Part of it runs through Ohio. Details can be found at http://northcountrytrail.org.

Cabins, Cottages, Yurts, and More

Camping, by definition, involves staying in a tent, RV, or perhaps an Adirondack-style shelter. For most people, that is. For some, staying in a cabin or a cottage or something of the sort also qualifies. And Ohio, primarily through its state park system, offers those kinds of opportunities.

One of the real benefits of this kind of "camping" is tied to the seasons. Many of these facilities remain open year-round, and so are popular with people looking for a place to stay—and a place where they can get warm—while hunting, cross-country skiing, snowshoeing, or just exploring the woods in winter. But people use them year-round, for family gatherings or to stay with friends and family who can't or won't sleep in a tent.

These state park structures come in several forms: cabins, cottages, yurts, teepees, and lodges.

Camper Cabins

These sleep up to four people on cots, bunks, or bench beds and come in two kinds. Regular camper cabins come with a cooler and camp light. Deluxe camper cabins also have some cooking equipment, including a mini refrigerator, microwave, camp stove, or outdoor grill. Some even come with TVs, ceiling fans, air conditioning, gas fireplaces, and porches.

Cottages

These are a step up from cabins and again come in various styles. Basic cottages sleep four and come with a complete kitchen, bath with shower, furnished living and dining areas, and cable or satellite TV. Towels, bed linens, dishes, and cookware are provided. They're open spring through fall. Preferred cottages have all of that plus a gas log fireplace and VCR or DVD player. They're available year-round. Premium cottages have two gas fireplaces, a hot tub, and Florida room. Family cottages are available throughout the year, too, and sleep six in two private bedrooms. They have heat and air conditioning and screened porch.

Cedar Cabins and Rent-a-RV

These are similar facilities in two shapes. Both are meant to make you feel like you're at home.

Cedar cabins have a private bedroom and a loft and can sleep four to six. They have a complete kitchen, private bathroom with shower or tub, furnished dining and living areas, air conditioning, and a porch or deck. Deluxe cedar cabins have all that and cookware, dishes, and linens.

Some state park cabins and cottages come with equipment like lanterns and stoves so that you don't have to bring your own, as is the case at Barkcamp State Park.

Rent-a-RVs are just what they suggest: complete, fully equipped, self-contained RV units. Some come with an outside grill.

Yurts and Tepees

So what exactly is a yurt? That's the first thing most people ask about these funny-looking abodes.

Yurts are circular cottages, you might say, descended from similar structures used by nomads in Mongolia, Turkey, and other parts of the world centuries ago. The sides back then were made of animal skins and the whole thing was made to be put and taken down over and over, as tribes moved around in the search for food. The Plains Indians of the American West operated the same way using tepees. You can stay in either at some state parks.

The yurts have canvas skins on wooden platforms. They come furnished with convertible futon beds and bunks, a table and chairs, mini-refrigerator or cooler, and internal electric outlets. Each site comes with a picnic table and fire ring, too. Some locations may also offer a range or camp stove, microwave or gas grill, sink with cold-running water, or a deck.

The tepees are also canvas on wooden frames. They sleep up to six and come equipped with a picnic table, fire ring, and waist-high charcoal grill.

One-of-a-Kind Shelters

A handful of state parks rent unique facilities. South Bass Island has "cabents." With wooden walls and a canvas roof, they look like a cross between a cabin and a yurt. Kelleys Island has a yurt on an island, while Lake Hope and Pike Lake State Parks offer lodges. Tar Hollow has a residence camp.

Conference Centers

Several state parks have combination lodge/conference centers that are more like hotels than anything else. You get an individual room and access to swimming pools, restaurants, balconies, or patios, cable TV, and all the rest.

In all cases, you can get details on which parks offer which cabins, cottages and the like at www.dnr.state.oh.us/camps/campingoptions/tabid/202/default.aspx.

Other Options

Muskingum Watershed Conservancy District also rents cabins and cottages at four of its parks: Atwood Lake, Pleasant Hill, Seneca Lake, and Tappan Lake. Pleasant Hill also has a house for rent. All are open year-round and can be rented by the day or week. Information is available at www.mwcd.org/recreation/camping-and-cabins.

Public-Private Partnership

There's one other option to keep in mind. American Electric Power owns 60,000 acres in southeastern Ohio. It's private property; the company is a publicly-traded corporation, one of the nation's largest generators of electricity.

It does, though, allow public use of that property. It was once extensively strip-mined. It's been reclaimed since, with 63 million trees planted and 600 lakes created. That's why the company refers to it as its "ReCreation Land" project.

The public can hike, rides horses, hunt, fish and camp on the property after securing a free permit. For details, visit www.aepohio.com/info/recreation/ or call (614) 716-1000.

Trip Planning

If you're buying this book, chances are you've got some camping gear and know how to use it; you're just looking for the best places to stay.

But what if you're a beginner? Ohio has some places specifically for you.

The Department of Natural Resources offers rent-a-camp sites at seven state parks. Each rent-a-camp site has a tent, already erected and under a canopy—imagine a tent within a tent and you'll get the idea. Tents have two cots with sleeping pads and the sites have a cooler, camp light, and stove. The canopy extends to cover a picnic table and fire ring. Some parks offer a few extras, too.

They're wonderful if you've wanted to try camping—especially for your children's sake—but didn't know how or where to get started or just don't have any equipment. Barkcamp, Blue Rock, Deer Creek, Kelleys Island, Lake Hope, Lake Loramie, and Maumee Bay offer rent-a-camp sites.

Wildlife

Ohio is home to a wide variety of wildlife, including mammals, like beavers, white-tailed deer, muskrats, gray squirrels, gray and red foxes, and birds, including barred owls, wood ducks, turkey vultures, and red-headed woodpeckers. There are plenty of places to see that wildlife, too. The state has eighty designated "watchable wildlife viewing sites." They're a mix of state-owned forests, wildlife areas and nature preserves, county and local parks, federal lands, and even some privately owned nature preserves. Some are open to hunting and fishing; others to nature viewing only. All have four common goals: to promote wildlife-associated recreation, economic development, education, and conservation. A visit to www.wildohio.com lets you find them all. There you can also buy a watchable wildlife viewing guide that gives you maps and directions to each site, details on what you might see there, and original artwork.

When visiting these places, keep a look out for some species of wildlife not native to the state that's become common. The coyote is one. Similar in looks to a medium-size dog, they're omnivores that will eat pretty much anything and can survive pretty much everywhere. They're spread across the state. Fox squirrels, rare when Ohio was extensively forested, have moved into the state and are expanding their range, too.

Other wildlife appears to be on its way back. The first settlers in Ohio would have found bobcats when they arrived. By 1850, though, the animals were gone, persecuted to the point of extirpation. They are still officially listed as threatened. But between 1970 and 2009 there were 359 verified reports of bobcats in the state; ninety-two of those occurred in 2009 alone.

It's another animal that once lived here but, until recently, has been long gone that's attracting the most attention lately. That's the black bear. As with the bobcat, bears were gone from Ohio by 1850. They remain a state endangered species. But whereas spotting one was unheard of even a decade ago, more and more people are seeing them these days. The Division of Wildlife estimated there were about sixty bears living in the state year-round as of 2011. Most sightings occurred in northeast and southeast Ohio, given that the bears seem to be moving into the state from neighboring Pennsylvania and West Virginia.

Most bears are spotted between May and August, when "dispersal" occurs. That's what they call it when a female bear kicks out her one-and-a-half-year-old cubs so that she can breed and raise a new litter. Those juveniles on their own for the first time tend to show up in all sorts of places—and get themselves into the public eye— as they look for a territory to call their own. Geauga County accounts for more sightings than any other, followed closely by Ashtabula, but black bears have been spotted in thirty-two counties all told.

Simply put, the population seems to be growing and expanding its territory, so if black bears aren't in your favorite campground yet, just wait. They may show up sooner rather than later.

Black bears are not typically aggressive. But they are big, serious animals, capable of scrambling up a tree like a raccoon and sprinting like a racehorse, so you don't want to treat them as harmless either. And they can become troublesome if they get used to eating human food. You definitely don't want them in your tent. In states where they are more common, wildlife officials tell you to pack not only your food, but also anything sweet smelling, like toothpaste and deodorant, in your vehicle when preparing for bed or otherwise closing up your campsite at night.

If you do encounter a bear that's being too inquisitive or that's making you feel uncomfortable, consider these tips from the Game Commission in Pennsylvania, which has about 18,000 black bears statewide:

- Stay Calm. If you see a bear and it hasn't seen you, leave the area calmly. Talk to the bear while moving away to help it discover your presence. Choose a route that will not intersect with the bear if it is moving.

- Get Back. If you have surprised a bear, slowly back away while quietly talking. Face the bear, but avoid direct eye contact. Do not turn and run; rapid movement may be perceived as danger to a bear that is already feeling threatened or may trigger a prey response. Avoid blocking the bear's only escape route and try to move away from any cubs you see or hear. Do not attempt to climb a tree. A female bear could interpret this as an attempt to get at her cubs, even though they may be in a different tree. Besides, black bears can climb better than you can.

- Pay Attention. If a bear is displaying signs of nervousness or discomfort with your presence, such as pacing, swinging its head, or popping its jaws, leave the area. Some bears may bluff charge to within a few feet. If this occurs, stand your ground, wave your arms wildly above your head to make yourself appear as big as possible, and shout at the bear. Turning and running could elicit a chase and you

Ohio is home to a lot of wildlife, with raccoons like these seen peeking from a tree in Lake Vesuvius Recreation Area among the most common.

cannot outrun a bear. Bears that appear to be stalking you should be confronted and made aware of your willingness to defend yourself by waving your arms and yelling while you continue to back away.

- Fight Back. If a bear attacks, fight back as you continue to leave the area. Bears have been driven away with rocks, sticks, binoculars, car keys, or even bare hands.

Generally, you can stay safe and enjoy wildlife without problems by treating the animals as the wild creatures they are. That means leaving bears, skunks, raccoons, and other critters to feed themselves. I'll never forget the time my wife, Mandy, and I took the kids camping and, just after crawling into the tent to unroll our sleeping bags, looked out to see four skunks just feet away. They were feeding on a bunch of sunflower seeds the previous camper had dumped on the ground at the base of a tree that was very near our tent door. We hadn't seen the seeds when setting up, but the skunks found them and by the time they'd had their fill and wandered away, the kids were asleep and we'd lost our evening.

The thing to remember in all cases is to let wildlife be wild. Animals that become habituated to people often get into trouble and end up being orphaned, relocated, or even killed. You can view wildlife, look at it, ooh and ah over it, love it, respect it, drool over it, but keep your hands off. That's the best thing for the animals in the long run.

Fishing and Hunting

Given the presence of all that wildlife, it's no surprise that Ohio has a strong hunting and fishing tradition. Roughly 800,000 people fish in the Buckeye State each year, while half a million or so go hunting.

But there are licenses required.

Hunters need licenses and sometimes more than one, depending on what they're chasing. Everyone needs a general license, but if you want to hunt deer, turkeys or waterfowl, or trap furbearers, you'll need licenses specific for those things. Residents buy licenses on an annual basis, with youth licenses available for those seventeen and younger and senior licenses for those sixty-six and older. Nonresidents can buy annual or three-day tourist licenses. Details on costs can be found at www.ohiodnr.com/wildlife/dow/regulations/hunting_licenses.aspx.

While you're online be sure to check out the maps of public wildlife areas available from the state's Division of Wildlife. These lands are public places purchased for the dual purposes of providing habitat for wildlife and open space for hunters to hunt. A list of them can be found at www.dnr.state.oh.us/Home/wild_resourcessubhome page/WildlifeAreaMaps/tabid/19694/Default.aspx.

Click on any area and you get not only a map, but details on what game species exist to be hunted and trapped and in what abundance, the best spots on that particular wildlife area to look for them, a list of facilities like latrines and parking lots, and more. There's also information on the state's toll-free Turn In a Poacher, or TIP, line where you can anonymously report violations or unsafe behavior. It's 1-800-POACHER.

Similar maps exist for fishermen at www.dnr.state.oh.us/Home/FishingSub homePage/LakeMapLandingPage/tabid/19478/Default.aspx. Focusing on lakes, reservoirs, and rivers, they provide general directions to the waterway and information on facilities like launch ramps, offer specifics on the kind of fish available to be caught, the size of fish most commonly caught at that water, the prospects for fishing by species, and tips on how, when and where to catch fish. There's contact information for the nearest division of wildlife office, too.

Anglers sixteen to sixty-five need a general fishing license. Kids fifteen and younger fish for free; those sixty-six and older can get a senior license. Nonresidents can get an annual license or three- or one-day tourist licenses. Residents and nonresidents alike can opt to buy a one-day Lake Erie charter license, too.

Ohio fishing and hunting licenses can be purchased online or at participating vendors, such as sporting goods stores, hardware stores, campgrounds and the like. You can find a list by county at www.ohiodnr.com/wildlife/dow/regulations/vendor.aspx.

Boating

Many of Ohio's public campgrounds are on or around rivers, streams, or lakes. That makes it easy to combine a campout with boating. There are some rules to remember, though.

Ohio's many reservoirs are home to fish from largemouth bass and bluegills to walleyes and catfish, like this flathead catfish caught after dark.

All boats need to be registered in Ohio; those 14 feet and longer also need to be titled. Certain bodies of water have specific rules unique to them. Some lakes have horsepower restrictions. Boating on Lake Erie requires you to carry more safety equipment, like flares, than elsewhere in the state. On lakes managed by the US Army Corps Pittsburgh District, everyone must wear a life jacket at all times when in canoes, kayaks, and other watercraft less than 16 feet in length. Ohio law requires children younger than ten to wear them at all times statewide when in boats less than 18 feet in length. Everyone, regardless of age, has to wear them while waterskiing or being towed behind a boat and while riding a personal watercraft.

Where to boat? The Department of Natural Resources offers information on its website at www.ohiodrr.com/watercraft. If you're a paddler, pay special attention to the list of rivers and streams and the list of water trails. The former details all of the state's popular paddling streams; the latter details those that have been marked and plotted just like hiking trails. Trail guides for each show access points for getting on and off the water, identify riffles, rapids and other potential hazards, point out historic sites you'll pass along the way and provide information about the fish to be caught and the wildlife to be seen.

No matter where you boat, consider taking a boating safety education class before your first venture. Successfully passing the class is a prerequisite for operating a motorboat for anyone born after 1982. More important, for everyone, the course will teach

A pair of anglers rest in their boat off the shore at Hueston Woods State Park. Boaters need to be aware of the rules pertaining to the water they're on.

you the "rules of the road" on the water and perhaps save your life.

Finally, be sure to clean all of your boating gear—as well as your fishing equipment—before moving from one waterway to another. That will help slow the spread of aquatic-invasive species.

To do your part, drain your boat or bilge of any water before you leave a site. Wash your gear—boats, life jackets, anchors and line, skis and tubes, live wells, bait buckets, paddles, waders, shoes and such—in water that's been heated to at least 140 degrees. If hot water isn't available, using a pressure washer at a commercial car wash is a good alternative. Be sure to completely dry any gear before moving from one waterway to another. Remove any visible mud, plants, and animals from your gear, but don't rely exclusively on a visible inspection. Some of these invasive species can exist and move about as a single cell, so a visual test alone isn't good enough.

Camping with Kids

There are all kinds of real, tangible benefits—mental, physical and social—to getting children outdoors and exploring nature, and it's just great fun, too. The memories you'll make fishing, paddling a canoe, hiking a trail, investigating leaves and bugs that you find, or counting the stars with your children are ones you will cherish forever.

There are some things you'll want to keep in mind to make any outing a successful one, though.

- Get the kids involved. Long before you leave home, allow the kids to help plan your "adventure." Look at park maps before you go and get the kids involved with picking a campground and a site within it. Ask what they want to do while they are there and then work together to pack everything from your fishing equipment to sleeping bags. Giving kids some ownership of the trip builds excitement.

- Get them their own gear. From a practical standpoint, you might be able to light up your campsite with one lantern. But the kids will have more fun if you let them each wear their own headlamp or carry their own flashlight, water bottle, or small backpack. You need not spend a lot of money on their gear initially; they'll outgrow some of it anyway. But if they have their own "stuff," they are more likely to feel like a camper.

- Keep it simple. As adults, we sometimes get hard core. We want to bike a top trail or fish a famous stream or marvel at a spectacular overlook. Kids want to have fun, too, but their attention spans are shorter. Keep that in mind when you go camping and let them set the pace. They may fish for an hour, then tire of it and want to hit the playground. A thirty-minute hike might be better for them than a day-long trek. Canoeing around the lake might need to be broken up with time spent looking for bugs. Remember, you're out here to get away from schedules. Be flexible.

- Explore the little things. When you camp with kids, it's always a good idea to spend time looking for fancy rocks, bugs, pinecones, and animal tracks. All of nature is new to children; be sure to discover it with them. And be enthusiastic about their finds. You want to build excitement in them, so make mudpies, build forts out of sticks, and search for feathers.

- Take more than one. The goal on any camping trip with children is to make sure they have fun; that will make them want to come back for more. So consider letting your children take along a friend. They'll keep each other occupied and happy.

- Make food fun. The old standby, the hot dog cooked on a stick over a fire, may not be the most appealing thing to the chefs among us, but kids love fires and cooking over them. Let them be involved and let them make things they don't get to make at home. Mountain pies are great, as are s'mores. One of those ice cream makers that you work by shaking is fun, too.

- Let others help. Many parks offer environmental education programs aimed specifically at children. Call ahead to the park you'll be visiting and see what they offer. Even if there's not a program scheduled per se, sometimes you can make arrangements to stop by a nature center and spend time with a ranger or educator who can let children touch animal hides, tell you where in the park to see wildlife, or otherwise help gain kids' interest.

- Have fun. The most important thing to remember when camping is to have fun. If you stress out on a campout or complain about how far the bathroom is from

Making kids a part of any camping outing is key to their having fun. Be sure to make time for activities, even if they involve getting sticky or muddy.

the tent or whine about sleeping on the ground, the kids will feed off that vibe. It's up to you to set the tone. When my children were little, we never went on "walks." We always went on "adventures" because the idea was to make them understand being outdoors was a grand experience, something to be cherished. Be positive. Be adventurous. Be fun.

So gather up the gang, grab your fishing rods and swimming suits, put on your sunscreen, and head outdoors. You'll be glad you did.

Tourism Information and Things to See and Do

In many cases, the parks surrounding your public campground will have plenty to keep you busy. There will be swimming, hiking, fishing, playgrounds, boating, and more. But that's not all there is to the state. There are many, many state and federal parks and wildlife refuges worth exploring, historic sites and museums focusing on everything from the Ohio River and old forts to aerospace to petroglyphs. You can even visit the prison used in the making of the *Shawshank Redemption*.

Telling you about them all is the job of Ohio's travel and tourism department. You can check out its website at discoverohio.com.

Exploring that website is especially worthwhile if you're looking to do a multi-day, multi-park camping excursion. It details road trips of interest so that the drive between parks can be fun and filled with places to eat, shop and explore. There's a suggested tour of Amish Country, for example, and others focusing on beaches, nature, and wineries. You can also get directions, special deals, and details on events like fairs, festivals, craft shows, and museums.

You may already know what you want to do and where, and that's OK. But a visit to the website may reveal opportunities you were not aware of, even close to the campground you've been visiting for years. It's worth a look anyway!

Brandywine Falls at Cuyahoga Valley National Park draws tourists to Ohio. The state is home to an abundance of sites worth seeing, both natural and historic.

Camping Etiquette

In our Boy Scout troop, we have a mantra: Leave every campsite better than you found it. Too few people live up to that standard. If you've ever pulled into your campsite, wanted to build a fire, and had to first empty the fire circle of bars of soap, toothpaste tubes, Styrofoam plates that didn't burn or melt, scraps of aluminum foil, those chemical handwarmers and the like, or had to clean your tent pad of food wrappers, plastic cups, and other debris, you know what I mean.

Nobody wants to have to clean up after the previous camper, so either dispose of your garbage—many campgrounds have a common Dumpster—or at least bag it up and take it out with you.

Here are some "Leave No Trace" principles to keep in mind:

- Plan ahead and prepare.
- Know the regulations and special concerns for the area you'll visit.
- Prepare for extreme weather, hazards, and emergencies.
- Schedule your trip to avoid times of high use.
- Visit in small groups when possible. Consider splitting larger groups into smaller ones.
- Repackage food to minimize waste.
- Use a map and compass to eliminate the use of marking paint, rock cairns, or flagging.
- Travel and camp on durable surfaces such as established trails and campsites, rock, gravel, dry grasses, or snow.
- Protect riparian areas by camping at least 200 feet from lakes and streams.
- Don't alter a site. Good campsites are found, not made.
- In popular areas, concentrate use on existing trails and campsites.
- Walk single file in the middle of the trail, even when it's wet or muddy.
- Keep campsites small. Focus activity in areas without vegetation.
- Disperse use in pristine areas to prevent creating new campsites and trails; avoid places where impacts are just beginning.
- Dispose of waste properly. Pack it in, pack it out. Inspect your campsite and rest areas for trash or spilled foods. Pack out all trash, leftover food, and litter.
- If you are somewhere without restrooms, deposit solid human waste in cat holes dug 6 to 8 inches deep at least 200 feet from water, campsites, and trails. Cover and disguise the cat hole when finished.
- Pack out toilet paper and other hygiene products.
- To wash yourself or your dishes, carry water 200 feet away from streams or lakes and use small amounts of biodegradable soap. Scatter strained dishwater.

A family plays on the beach at Caesar Creek State Park. Rules at parks and their campgrounds are important to follow for a safe and fun experience.

- Leave what you find. Preserve the past: examine, but do not touch, cultural or historic structures and artifacts.
- Leave rocks, plants, and other natural objects as you find them.
- Avoid introducing or transporting non-native species.
- Do not build structures or furniture, or dig trenches.
- Minimize campfires, which can cause lasting impacts to the backcountry. Use a lightweight stove for cooking and enjoy a candle lantern for light.
- Where fires are permitted, use established fire rings, fire pans, or mound fires.
- Keep fires small. Only use sticks from the ground that can be broken by hand.
- Burn all wood and coals to ash, put out campfires completely, then scatter cool ashes.
- Respect wildlife by observing it from a distance. Do not follow or approach it.
- Never feed wild animals. Feeding wildlife damages their health, alters natural behaviors, and exposes them to predators and other dangers.
- Protect wildlife and your food by storing rations and trash securely.
- Avoid wildlife during sensitive times: mating, nesting, raising young, or winter.
- Be courteous. Yield to other users on the trail.
- Step to the downhill side of the trail when encountering pack stock.

- Take breaks and camp away from trails and other visitors.
- Let nature's sounds prevail. Avoid loud voices and noises.
  For more information visit www.LNT.org.

In addition to these guidelines, be considerate of your neighbors and observe the posted quiet times within a campground. The rules don't say you have to go to bed at a particular time. But if quiet time is 10 p.m. to 6 a.m., don't be hooting and hollering at 2 a.m. Don't monopolize the facilities either. If you've got wet clothes, for example, string a clothesline rather than draping them over the bathroom facilities everyone has to share.

And if you've got the family dog along, and the rules say he must be leashed, don't turn him loose to roam the campground. Your pet not only could get hurt by a passing vehicle, but also could ruin the stay of others.

Map Legend

Interstate Highway

US Highway

State Highway

International Border

State Border

Region Boundary

River or Creek

Body of Water

Capital

Campground

Town

Northeast

So how do you like your fun? No matter what the answer is, chances are northeast Ohio has something for you.

There are interesting parks to explore. Pymatuning State Park, shared with Pennsylvania, offers terrific walleye fishing. It's gotten so good lately that Ohio Division of Wildlife biologists have been touting it as a go-to water. Shenango River Lake, a US Army Corps of Engineers facility nearby, is another favorite of boaters and anglers. The waterway that stands out above all others, though, is Lake Erie. One of the five Great Lakes, it fronts the northernmost edge of this region almost completely from east to west. Just two parks with campgrounds front the lake directly, one of them tiny. But opportunities to get on the water are plentiful.

A little farther south is Cuyahoga Valley National Park. It's the only national park within the state offering camping, and it's big on history. The opportunity to combine a hike or bike trip with a ride on a vintage train is not to be missed. If that doesn't do it for you, how about the opportunity to camp at a state park that doubles as a working farm? You can find that here, too.

There are a number of state forests, some of which have been in state hands for quite a while. Others are of more recent vintage. All are wonderful for hiking, fishing, and hunting. Equestrians love them with good reason. There are miles upon miles of bridle trails begging to be explored.

Away from the woods, the Rock and Roll Hall of Fame and Museum is in this corner of the state, as is the Pro Football Hall of Fame. There are art and railroad museums, a casino, and the Cleveland Zoo. The Great Lakes Science Center is here. The First Ladies National Historic Site, which pays tribute to the contributions of presidential wives, is as well, fittingly considering that Ohio has produced eight presidents. This is also where much of Ohio's Amish population is centered, so if you want to sample some of their food and crafts, you can find it.

Take all of that together—the natural attractions, the museums and wineries, the arts, even the professional sports teams in Cleveland—and there is sure to be something for everyone in your group. Pick a campground and have at it!

1

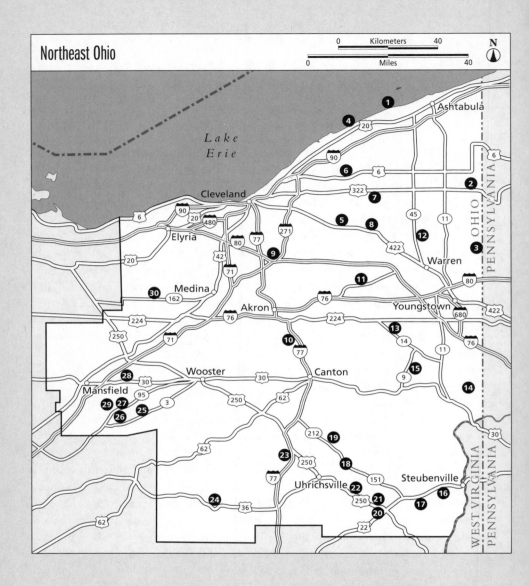

Northeast Ohio

Erie's Shores and More

	total sites	hookups	max RV lengths	toilets	showers	drinking water	dump station	recreation	fee	reservation
1 Geneva State Park	100	Y	45	F	Y	Y	Y	HBFSEEU	$$$$	Y
2 Pymatuning State Park	352	Y	50	F	Y	Y	Y	HBFSLU	$$$$	Y
3 Shenango River Lake Recreation Area	330	Y	76	F	Y	Y	Y	HBFSLUO	$$$–$$$$	Y
4 Perry Township Park	20	Y	38	F	Y	Y	N	HBFS	$–$$$$	Y
5 Punderson State Park	194	Y	60	F	Y	Y	Y	HBFSC	$$$$	Y
6 Big Creek Park	4	N/A	N/A	V	N	N	N	HFR	$$$$	Y
7 Headwaters Park	6	N/A	N/A	V	N	N	N	HBFCR	$$$$	Y
8 Chickagami Park	12	N/A	N/A	V	N	N	N	HCR	$$$$	Y
9 Cuyahoga Valley National Park	5	N/A	N/A	V	N	Y	N	HCEE	$$$	Y
10 Portage Lakes State Park	74	Y	40	V	N	Y	Y	HBFSLU	$$$$	Y
11 West Branch State Park	198	Y	50	F	Y	Y	Y	HBFSCLRU	$$$$	Y
12 Mosquito Lake State Park	234	Y	50	F	Y	Y	Y	HBFSCLRU	$$$$	Y
13 Berlin Lake	347	Y	82	F	Y	Y	Y	HBFLU	$$$–$$$$	Y
14 Beaver Creek State Park	109	Y	25	V	N	Y	Y	HBFSCLRU	$$$$	Y
15 Guilford Lake State Park	41	Y	40	F	Y	Y	Y	HBFSU	$$$$	Y
16 Fernwood State Forest	22	N	N/A	V	N	N	N	HFU	N/A	N
17 Friendship Park	14	Y	50	V	N	Y	Y	HBFCRU	$$$	Y
18 Leesville Southfork Campground	75	Y	50	V	N	Y	Y	HBFU	$$$$	Y
19 Atwood Lake Park	600	Y	35	F	Y	Y	Y	HBFSLU	$$$$	Y
20 Sally Buffalo Park	300	Y	N/A	F	Y	Y	Y	HBFSC	$$$–$$$$	Y
21 Harrison State Forest	27	N	N/A	V	N	Y	N	HRU	N/A	N
22 Tappan Lake Park	500	Y	35	F	Y	Y	Y	HBFSLEEU	$$$$	Y
23 Tuscarawas County Fairgrounds	200	Y	N/A	F	Y	Y	Y	HF	$$–$$$	Y
24 Coshocton Lake Park	69	Y	40	F	Y	Y	Y	HSC	$$$$	Y
25 Mohican State Park	186	Y	50	F	Y	Y	Y	HBFCRU	$$$$	Y
26 Mohican-Memorial State Forest	10	N	N/A	V	N	Y	N	HCRU	N/A	N
27 Pleasant Hill Lake Park	417	Y	35	F	Y	Y	Y	HBFSLRU	$$$$	Y
28 Charles Mill Lake Park	500	Y	35	F	Y	Y	Y	HBFSLU	$$$$	Y
29 Malabar Farm State Park	15	N	50	V	N	Y	N	HF	$$$–$$$$	Y
30 Findley State Park	271	Y	50	F	Y	Y	Y	HBFSCLU	$$$$	Y

See fee codes on page xx and amenities codes on page xxiii.

1 Geneva State Park

Location: North of Geneva
Season: Year-round, facilities limited in winter
Sites: 100
Maximum RV length: 45 feet
Facilities: Flush toilets, warm showers, electricity, water, sanitary dump station, picnic tables, fire rings, coin-operated laundry, basketball and volleyball courts, fish-cleaning house, sports equipment available for loan to campers, environmental education programs, archery range, marina
Fee per night: $$$$
Pets: Permitted at some sites
Activities: Boating, hiking, fishing, swimming, hunting, shooting
Management: Ohio Department of Natural Resources
Contact: (440) 446-8400; www.dnr.state.oh.us/parks/parks/geneva/tabid/736/Default.aspx. For reservations call (866) 644-6727 or visit www.ohio.reserveworld.com.
Finding the campground: From Geneva, head north on SR 534. Go 3.1 miles, then turn left onto Lake Road West. Go 2 miles to the campground.
GPS coordinates: N 41 51.222'/ W 80 58.689'
Other: This park rents a dozen deluxe cedar cabins and is home to Geneva-on-the-Lake, the state park system's ninth resort and conference center. It has 109 rooms.
About the campground: The campground is a couple of loops. The fish-cleaning house is adjacent to the loop that holds campsites 1 to 37. The full-service campsites are in an adjacent loop.
Why it's worth a visit: The obvious draw here is the park's location on the shores of Lake Erie. It fronts the lake for about 2 miles. Campers have access—via a marina with a six-lane boat ramp—to the lake and its central basin, an area that fishermen from far and wide target to catch walleyes above all else, but also yellow perch, catfish, and steelhead. You need not bring your own boat, though. There are numerous charters based here. If it's not fishing you're into, the park has a natural sand beach for swimming, several areas of freshwater marsh, and some mature woods. You can explore that using 8 miles of trails, 2 of them paved for non-motorized bikes. That varied habitat means you can find some plants that are more commonly found on the Atlantic coast than in Ohio, species such as sea rocket, seaside spurge, beach pea, swamp smartweed, and leafy sedge. Bird life is varied and abundant, too, so bring your binoculars and camera.

2 Pymatuning State Park

Location: Southwest of Andover
Season: Mid-Apr–Nov
Sites: 352, some walk-in only
Maximum RV length: 50 feet
Facilities: Flush toilets, warm showers, electricity, water, sanitary dump station, laundry facility, camp store, nature center, environmental education programming, playground, basketball and volleyball courts, boat launch, free WiFi access at camp office for campers
Fee per night: $$$$

Pets: Permitted in some sites

Activities: Swimming, boating, fishing, hiking, hunting

Management: Ohio Department of Natural Resources

Contact: (440) 293-6030 park office; (440) 293-6684 campground office; www.dnr.state.oh.us/parks/parks/pymatuning/tabid/781/Default.aspx. For reservations call (866) 644-6727 or visit www.ohio.reserveworld.com.

Finding the campground: From Andover, follow SR 85/East Main Street east for 1.5 miles. Turn right onto Pymatuning Lake Road/CR 274 and go 1.7 miles to the campground.

GPS coordinates: N 41 32.901' / W 80 31.787'

Other: This park rents twenty-three family cottages, thirty-two standard cottages and three yurts.

About the campground: This is a mega-campground, with lots and lots of sites packed so close together that your shadow will fall on family, friends and neighbors. The premium sites with full service are also those closest to the lake, with shoreline views. Some sites can be rented for the entire season.

Why it's worth a visit: When it comes to Pymatuning it's all—or at least mostly—about the fishing. Pymatuning Lake covers about 17,000 acres and offers some of the finest walleye, crappie, bass, channel catfish, and musky fishing in all of Ohio. The lake straddles the Ohio-Pennsylvania border. That means there are some unique rules to keep in mind, though. The two states have agreed to limit boat motors to 20 horsepower and, so long as you are in a boat, you can fish anywhere with a fishing license from either state. If you are on shore, you need a license from that state. As for where on this giant lake to start, a call to the Ohio Division of Natural Resources at (330) 644-2293 will get you not only a map of Pymatuning Lake and the site of man-made habitat structures, but also GPS coordinates for those hot spots. While you're here, head east to Pennsylvania and check out its facilities. Near the town of Linesville you can visit a wildlife visitor center and see bald eagles, check out a state-run fish hatchery and, most impressively, see the thousands of carp that gather at the spillway in such numbers that "ducks walk on the fish's backs."

3 Shenango River Lake Recreation Area

Location: South of Greenville, Pa.

Season: Mid-May–early Sept

Sites: 330

Maximum RV length: 76 feet

Facilities: Flush toilets, warm showers, sanitary dump station, water, electricity, picnic tables, fire rings, boat launches, off-road vehicle area

Fee per night: $$$ to $$$$

Pets: Leashed pets permitted

Activities: Boating, hiking, fishing, hunting, waterskiing, tubing, swimming, off-road riding

Management: US Army Corps of Engineers, Pittsburgh District

Contact: (724) 962-7746; www.lrp.usace.army.mil/rec/lakes/shenango.htm. Reservations can be made by calling toll free (877) 444-6777 or visiting www.recreation.gov. There are some first come, first served campsites.

Visitors feed the carp and geese at the famous spillway on the Pennsylvania side of Pymatuning State Park.

Finding the campground: From Greenville, follow SR 18 south. Just before crossing the bridge over Shenango Reservoir, turn right onto West Lake Road and go about 1.25 miles to the campground.

GPS coordinates: N 41 17.879' / W 80 25.874'

Other: History buffs will enjoy exploring the remnants of the Erie Extension Canal, which played a key role in the economic development of this part of the world. Sections of it are located here and maintained for hiking as part of the Shenango Trail. The well-preserved remains of Lock Number 10 are found in Sharpsville, Pennsylvania, a half mile downstream of the dam. Another historic feature worth checking out is the Kidd's Mill Covered Bridge.

About the campground: Group camping is available at the Big Bend Access area.

Why it's worth a visit: It allows unlimited horsepower boating. That makes it very popular for waterskiing, tubing and fishing. For a different experience, though, take your canoe or kayak and explore some of the lake's more remote areas. You can also go upstream and float the Shenango River. A water trail has been developed from Pymatuning State Park to Greenville on the Pennsylvania side; plans are to extend it down to this recreation area next. Now that some of the fallen timber and brush has been removed this is a nice, relaxing Class I float suitable for paddlers. Another thing that makes this park unique is the presence of the Bayview Off-Road Vehicle Area for all-terrain vehicles. It's open from late May through the end of September. There are some rules to follow: there's no riding by anyone younger than eight, and those eight to fifteen must pass a safety education course. But meet those standards and this is a good place to ride.

4 Perry Township Park

Location: North of Perry

Season: May 1–Oct 31

Sites: 20

Maximum RV length: 38 feet

Facilities: Showers, flush toilets, water, electricity, picnic tables, fire rings, boat launch, baseball and soccer fields, tennis courts, playground, community center

Fee per night: $ to $$$$

Pets: Leashed pets permitted

Activities: Boating, fishing, hiking, swimming, sports activities

Management: Perry Township

Contact: For reservations call (440) 259-5957; www.perrytownship-lake.com/.

Finding the campground: From Perry, head north on Center Road for 0.5 mile. Turn left onto Middle Ridge Road, go 0.2 mile, then take a slight left onto US 20/North Ridge Road and go 0.7 mile. Take the first right onto Perry Park Road and go 1.4 miles to the park entrance, then follow signs to CAMPGROUND.

GPS coordinates: N 41 47.724' / W 81 09.753'

Other: Alcoholic beverages are prohibited. Having them in the park or campground is cause for dismissal.

About the campground: Weekly, monthly and seasonal passes are available to RV campers. Tent campers can only stay on a short-term basis.

Why it's worth a visit: This park is located right on Lake Erie's shore, so access to that Great Lake is the main draw. There's a boat launch; its use is restricted to township residents and campers, so staying here gives you the benefit of its use. The park's heavily-wooded 70 acres open up onto the water, offering great beach scenes, scattered driftwood and plenty of wildlife. Be sure to bring a camera. The amount and variety of waterfowl and shorebirds can be amazing at certain times of year, with species that are otherwise scarce passing through. The steep, 30-foot-tall bluffs here are especially dramatic. A hiking trail that leads through them is the best way to experience what they are all about. Fishing can be excellent, with walleyes, smallmouth bass, crappies, and yellow perch among the species often caught, sometimes in abundance.

5 Punderson State Park

Location: East of Garfield Heights
Season: May–Dec
Sites: 194
Maximum RV length: 60 feet
Facilities: Flush toilets, warm showers, electricity, water and sewage, sanitary dump station, picnic tables, fire rings, water, nature center, environmental education programming, camp store, laundry facilities, sports equipment available for loan, golf course, archery range, tennis courts, disc golf course
Fee per night: $$$$
Pets: Permitted at some sites
Activities: Boating, hiking, biking, fishing, swimming, golfing
Management: Ohio Department of Natural Resources
Contact: (440) 564-2279 park office; (440) 564-1195 campground office; www.dnr.state.oh.us/ parks/parks/punderson/tabid/780/Default.aspx. For reservations call (866) 644-6727 or visit www.ohio.reserveworld.com.
Finding the campground: From Garfield Heights, head east on I-480 for 4.7 miles. Keep left to take I-480 North toward I-271 and Erie via ext 26 and go 1.5 miles. Take the I-271 local lanes north and exit on the left toward US 422 west/Harvard/Chagrin, go 0.7 mile, then merge onto I-271 north and go 1.5 miles. Take exit 29 for US 422/SR 87/Chagrin Road, go 0.3 mile, turn right onto Chagrin Road/SR 87 and go 1.3 miles. Take the third exit onto Pinetree Road East/SR 87 and go 1 mile. Take a slight right onto South Woodland Road/SR 87 and go 2.3 miles, then turn left to stay on SR 87. Go 9.7 miles to the park entrance and look for the signs to CAMPGROUND.
GPS coordinates: N 41 27.675' / W 81 13.166'
Other: The campground is situated on the site of a former Indian village. It's also home to a lodge and conference center with thirty-one guest rooms, twenty-six cottages and an organized group camping area.
About the campground: This is a large campground with a lot of sites, so don't expect too much in the way of privacy. There are some "hill" tent sites, though, that are essentially walk-in sites hidden behind trees and vegetation. A visit to the park website lets you see photos of each campsite.

Why it's worth a visit: There are not a lot of tall mountains in Ohio, so no one's going to confuse it with Vail. But Punderson is considered to be Ohio's premier winter park, with two cross-country ski trails, a lighted sledding hill, a mushers trail for dog sledders and three snowmobile trails. There are a couple of things to recommend this park in the warmer months, too. One is its golf course, which features 18 holes stretched over 6,800 yards. There are some especially long par 3 and 5 holes on the backside. Hole number 8 is the course's signature challenge, with a narrow and wooded downhill fairway and dogleg over a pond to the green. Another attraction is Punderson's natural features. It's got three lakes—Punderson Lake at 150 acres is the largest—that offer opportunities to fish and boat. There are also seven hiking trails and a multi-use trail. None are especially long, nor do they cover especially difficult terrain. But you can spend time looking for shorebirds, mammals like white-tailed deer and wildflowers like buttercup and wild geranium, then head to nearby Tinker's Creek and Nelson-Kennedy Ledges State Parks. Neither offer camping, but Tinker's Run has a nature reserve worth exploring and Nelson-Kennedy has some cliffs to visit.

6 Big Creek Park

Location: North of Chardon
Season: Year-round
Sites: 4, for tents only
Maximum RV length: N/A
Facilities: Vault toilets, fire rings, grills, picnic tables, water pump (though visitors are encouraged to bring their own water in case it's not working)
Fee per night: $$$$
Pets: Leashed pets permitted
Activities: Hiking, fishing, horseback riding
Management: Geauga County Parks District
Contact: For reservations call (440) 286-9516 or visit www.geaugaparkdistrict.org.
Finding the campground: From Chardon, follow North Street north for 0.8 mile. Continue straight another 0.7 mile as North Street becomes Ravenna Road. Turn right onto Woodin Road, go 0.8 mile, then turn left onto Robinson Road. Go about 1 mile, then turn left into the park and follow the signs for CAMPGROUND.
GPS coordinates: N 41 37.258' / W 81 12.083'
Other: This park also rents two lean-tos.
About the campground: The maximum stay here is five consecutive nights. Though it's open year-round, roads may not be plowed in winter.
Why it's worth a visit: Big Creek Park exists because of a failed dream. In 1926 Samuel Livingston Mather bought almost 1,000 acres with hopes of creating a high-class resort. The onset of the Great Depression crushed that. But, almost thirty years later, half of his original purchase was donated to the state to preserve open space. That donation was the start of Big Creek Park. It's grown so that today visitors can explore 642 acres of beech-maple woods, see brilliant wildflowers in spring and take in the views of scenic Big Creek, which bisects the park. A network of 6.4 miles of trails wind through the property. Some are for hiking, a couple are paved so as to be accessible to people with disabilities. The longest two trails, the Creek and Highline, were designed with

A bullfrog sits on the shores of one of the ponds at Big Creek Park in Geauga County.

equestrians in mind. A 1-mile section of the Buckeye Trail passes by the campground, too. Three ponds close to the campground offer fishing for bass and bluegills; catch and release is encouraged. There's a "Monarch Waystation" butterfly garden that attracts butterflies and hummingbirds all summer that's worth checking out.

7 Headwaters Park

Location: Northeast of Burton
Season: Year-round
Sites: 6, for tents only
Maximum RV length: N/A
Facilities: Vault toilets, fire rings, grills, picnic tables, boat launch, water pump (though visitors are encouraged to bring their own water in case it's not working)
Fee per night: $$$$
Pets: Leashed pets permitted
Activities: Hiking, mountain biking, fishing, horseback riding, boating, geocaching
Management: Geauga County Parks District
Contact: For reservations call (440) 286-9516 or visit www.geaugaparkdistrict.org.

Finding the campground: Follow Goodwin Avenue east for 3.4 miles. Turn left onto Old State Road/SR 608 and go about 2 miles, then turn right at the HEADWATERS PARK sign and follow the directions to the campground.

GPS coordinates: N 41 30.331' / W 81 06.095'

Other: This park also rents 1 lean-to.

About the campground: This campground is home to the one ADA-accessible site in the Geauga County park system. It's a 10-by-10 tent pad. Though the campground is open year-round, roads may not be plowed in winter.

Why it's worth a visit: Up until 1932, picnickers enjoyed summer afternoons in the ravine along the East Branch Cuyahoga River. Then the City of Akron bought the land and flooded it to create the East Branch Reservoir as a water supply impoundment. Twenty-plus years later, city officials opened the land around the lake as a park. That became Headwaters Park. It's got a lot to offer. The 420-acre lake is open to fishing for largemouth bass, northern pike, crappies, bluegills, and catfish, though shore access is limited to certain areas for the purpose of controlling erosion. Boating is allowed, too, with a 1.5-horsepower limit. This park is also popular with birders given the variety of species that either migrate through or stay year-round. Loons, tundra swans and ducks are common in spring and fall. Sandpipers and plovers visit in summer. A nesting platform built for ospreys has resulted in resident birds. The Pike Point and Kingfisher Trails lead to waterfowl observation areas where you can see a lot of birds. As for other hiking, more than 2 miles of the Buckeye Trail go through the park.

8 Chickagami Park

Location: East of Welshfield

Season: Year-round

Sites: 12, for tents only

Maximum RV length: N/A

Facilities: Vault toilets, fire rings, grills, picnic tables

Fee per night: $$$$

Pets: Leashed pets permitted

Activities: Hiking, mountain biking, horseback riding

Management: Geauga County Parks District

Contact: For reservations call (440) 286-9516; www.geaugaparkdistrict.org.

Finding the campground: From Welshfield, head east on US 422 for 4.2 miles. Turn left onto Madison Road/SR 88 and go 0.2 mile, then take the second left onto High Street/SR 168 and go 0.9 mile to the park entrance. From there follow the signs to CAMPGROUND.

GPS coordinates: N 41 22.901' / W 81 04.485'

Other: This park rents 3 lean-tos and has a group camping area.

About the campground: The group sites here are relatively new. The Boy Scouts retain exclusive use to some sites. Though the campground is open year-round, roads may not be plowed in winter.

Why it's worth a visit: This is one of the smaller parks in the Geauga County system at just 139 acres, most of it woods, with some wetlands, streams, and uplands mixed in. It's also the park with the greatest camping tradition. The name itself, Chickagami, is a Native American term meaning "camp by the lake." The Boy Scouts have been camping here since 1941. The Scouts' Western

Reserve Council owned the property and ran it as a scout camp until 2003, when the county bought the land. The Boy Scouts still make great use of the park, but the public is welcome, too. There's a large open field good for games and group activities and three trails. They total less than 1 mile in length, but plans are to add additional trails in the future. Until then, if you're willing to blaze your own way, there's a lot of wildlife to be seen, from songbirds like purple finches, pine warblers, and scarlet tanagers to white-tailed deer, turkeys, and raccoons.

9 Cuyahoga Valley National Park

Location: North of Akron
Season: Late May–Oct
Sites: 5
Maximum RV length: N/A
Facilities: Vault toilets, water, picnic tables, fire rings, historical and environmental education programming
Fee per night: $$$
Pets: Leashed pets permitted
Activities: Hiking, biking, museums
Management: Conservancy for Cuyahoga Valley National Park
Contact: Reach Cuyahoga Valley National Park at (330) 657-2752 or (800) 257-9477. Reservations are preferred 3 days in advance and can be made by contacting the Conservancy for Cuyahoga Valley National Park at (330) 657-2909, ext 119. Sites may be available to walk-up visitors, however. Details are available at www.conservancyforcvnp.org/experience/visit/places-to-stay.
Finding the campground: From Akron, follow SR 8 north for 10.8 miles. Take exit 12 toward SR 303 and go 0.2 mile, then turn left onto SR 303 3.5 miles. Turn right onto Riverview Road, go 1.6 miles, then turn right onto Boston Mills Road. Go 0.2 mile, then turn left onto Stanford Road and follow it to the Standford House, which is on the right.
GPS coordinates: N 41 16.252' / W 81 33.415'
Other: Visitors to this park who want to stretch their camping along the Towpath Trail can take advantage of shelters operated by two counties. Summit County permits camping year-round along the Towpath Trail at two primitive sites, one at the Big Bend Trailhead in Akron and a second about a quarter mile south of the Franklin Trailhead in New Franklin. Camping is permitted for one-night stays only and sites are available on a first-come, first-served basis. Reservations are not required. Call (330) 867-5511 or visit www.summitmetroparks.org/Activities/Camping.aspx. Farther south, Stark County operates the primitive Rivers Edge Camping Area along the Ohio & Erie Canal Towpath Trail near the Brideport Quarry Trailhead. Reservations are not required, but visitors must call (330) 353-2377 when they arrive. Visit www.starkparks.com/camping.asp.
About the campground: These are grassy sites on the edge of the woods. Sites are limited to two tents and six people each, and there's a maximum stay of ten consecutive nights. Fires are not permitted within individual sites; you have the use of the group fire ring.
Why it's worth a visit: Cuyahoga Valley National Park is a big one, taking in 33,000 acres along both sides of the Cuyahoga River. As you'd expect, there are a lot of things to do. One of the more interesting ways to see this park and to tie in a night or more at its campground is to use the

A family looks at Brandywine Falls from an observation deck in Cuyahoga Valley National Park.

Towpath Trail. This is a hard-packed, gravel multi-use trail that follows the route of the old Ohio and Erie Canal. Built between 1825 and 1832, the canal played a vital role in the settlement of the state by helping farmers get their goods to urban markets between Cleveland and Portsmouth. Today, hikers and bikers who use the trail can see some old remnants of the canal and visit four different visitor centers. They're all staffed by park rangers and packed with exhibits and interpretive information. It's near one of those, the Boston Store Visitor Center, where you come to the park's only tent camping facilities. Located behind the Stanford House, the small site is for bikers and long-distance hikers only. You can park no closer than the Boston Store Visitor Center. That makes for a quiet, peaceful setting with like-minded adventurers. You can make a visit here really fun by combining it with a ride on the Cuyahoga Valley Scenic Railroad. Operated by a nonprofit group, it's billed as one of the oldest, longest and most scenic tourist excursions in the country. Hikers and bikers can travel the Towpath Trail one way, then ride the train back the other. Visit www.CVSR.com for details.

10 Portage Lakes State Park

Location: South of Akron
Season: Apr–Dec
Sites: 74
Maximum RV length: 40 feet

Facilities: Vault toilets, electricity, sun shower (bring your own water bag), sanitary dump station, picnic tables, fire rings, water, basketball court, horseshoe pits, boat launch, playground
Fee per night: $$$$
Pets: Permitted at all sites
Activities: Boating, fishing, swimming, hiking, hunting
Management: Ohio Department of Natural Resources
Contact: (330) 644-2220; www.dnr.state.oh.us/parks/parks/portage/tabid/779/Default.aspx. For reservations call (866) 644-6727 or visit www.ohio.reserveworld.com.
Finding the campground: From Akron, head south on SR 8, continuing for 4.7 miles after it turns into I-77. Take the Arlington Road exit, exit 120, go 0.3 mile, and turn right onto South Arlington Road, continuing for 3.3 miles. Turn right on to East Nimisila Road, go 1.1 miles, then turn left onto Christman Road and follow the signs to CAMPGROUND.
GPS coordinates: N 40 56.470' / W 81 30.990'
Other: This park has two teepees for rent within the campground from May 1–Oct 31 and offers boat-in-only camping on Latham Bay.
About the campground: Just six of the sites at this campground have electricity. The campground does have its own boat launch and beach on Nimisila Reservoir, though. Some sites also front a smaller pond.
Why it's worth a visit: Portage Lakes State Park is well named. It has eight lakes of various sizes covering a total of 2,034 acres within its borders, compared to just 411 acres of solid ground. Two of the lakes, Turkeyfoot Lake and East Reservoir, allow powerboating for skiing and tubing at certain times of day. The other six are all operated under no-wake rules, with some—such as Nimisila Lake, which surrounds the campground—limited to electric motors only. Boaters will find several private marinas, eight boat launches, boat swim areas and boat rentals around the park. There are bass, walleyes, muskies, pickerel, catfish, and carp to be caught on rod and reel and a wheelchair access for fishermen on North Reservoir. Be sure to bring your binoculars when you visit. The wetlands and marshy areas of the park are home to all sorts of birds. Geese and ducks not only nest here, but migrate through by the thousands in spring and fall. And if you prefer to look skyward for other sights, the Astronomy Club of Akron runs a small observatory within the park; tours and programs are available.

11 West Branch State Park

Location: East of Ravenna
Season: Mid-Apr–Dec
Sites: 198, some ADA accessible
Maximum RV length: 50 feet
Facilities: Flush toilets, warm showers, electricity, laundry facilities, sanitary dump station, water, picnic tables, fire rings, sports equipment available for loan, boat launch, environmental education programming, marina, playgrounds, volleyball courts
Fee per night: $$$$
Pets: Permitted at all sites
Activities: Swimming, fishing, boating, hiking, mountain biking, horseback riding, hunting
Management: Ohio Department of Natural Resources

Contact: (330) 296-3239; www.dnr.state.oh.us/parks/parks/westbrnc/tabid/795/Default.aspx. For reservations call (866) 644-6727 or visit www.ohio.reserveworld.com.

Finding the campground: From Ravenna, follow SR 59 east for 2.1 miles. Stay straight to follow SR 5 east/Ravenna Road for 3 miles, then turn right onto Rock Spring Road and go another 0.3 mile. Take the first left onto Esworthy Road, go 1.2 miles and follow the signs.

GPS coordinates: N 41 08.451' / W 81 07.094'

Other: This park has an organized group tenting site near the 700-foot swimming beach, as well as an equestrian camping area with nine sites, vault latrines, a gray water station and a picket line, all near 20 miles of bridle trails.

About the campground: Located on a peninsula in Michael J. Kirwan Lake, this is a large campground with a lot of sites. There is not a lot of privacy, though the sites closest to the group camp sites are a little more secluded.

Why it's worth a visit: This is a huge chunk of country. The lake is nearly 2,700 acres, while the land around it takes in almost 5,400 acres of woods and fields. There's correspondingly a lot to do. The lake is open to boats with unlimited horsepower, so there are opportunities to ski and tube as well as fish and swim. There's a marina, accessible piers and beaches with changing stations to accommodate all of those activities. Mountain bikers love the park as much as anyone. That's because it has 12 miles of biking trails. Most started out as snowmobile trails, and they still get used for that purpose in winter. But in the warmer months there are single- and double-track trails for everyone from beginners to advanced, adventurous riders. Some of the trails are connected and can be done as loops. Maps available from the park allow you to plan out your trip.

12 Mosquito Lake State Park

Location: North of Warren

Season: May–Dec

Sites: 234, some walk-in only

Maximum RV length: 50 feet

Facilities: Flush toilets, electricity, warm showers, sanitary dump station, water, picnic tables, fire rings, boat launch, disc golf course, dog park, environmental education programs from Memorial Day weekend through Labor Day weekend, playground, basketball and volleyball courts, horseshoe pits

Fee per night: $$$$

Pets: Permitted in camping area 1, but not in area 2

Activities: Boating, fishing, swimming, hiking, mountain biking, horseback riding, disc golf, hunting

Management: Ohio Department of Natural Resources

Contact: (330) 637-2856 park office; (330) 638-5700 campground office; www.dnr.state.oh.us/parks/parks/mosquito/tabid/771/Default.aspx. For reservations call (866) 644-6727 or visit www.ohio.reserveworld.com. Some of the sites are first come, first served.

Finding the campground: From Warren, follow Elm Street/SR 5 northeast for 4.5 miles. Turn left onto Warren Meadville Road, go 0.5 mile and take the second left onto Durst Colebrook Road for 0.3 mile. Turn left onto Wilson Sharpsville Road/SR 305. Go about 1.2 miles, then turn right onto Hogland-Blackstub Road and follow signs to Campground.

GPS coordinates: N 41 19.021' / W 80 46.704'

Other: This campground rents two yurts, each of which has a raised porch and a lakeside view. There's also a boat launching area for campers with shoreline tie-ups.

About the campground: The majority of the sites are situated in a mature forest, though others provide lakeshore access and vistas.

Why it's worth a visit: Mosquito Lake is one of the largest lakes in Ohio, covering 7,850 acres. That makes it hugely popular with both boaters and anglers. Boaters, given the fact the lake has no horsepower limits, flock here for the chance to ski, tube, and run their personal watercraft. The park has a concessionaire that rents pontoons, fishing boats, and personal watercrafts. Fishermen pursue Mosquito Lake's abundant walleyes, bass, northern pike, and crappies. Five boat launches make getting on the water easy, while a full-service marina can supply your needs. Away from the lake, the park offers two miles of hiking-only trails and additional miles open to bikes and horses. While here, be on the lookout for unusual wildlife. The bears and wolves that roamed the area centuries ago are long gone, but otters were reintroduced into suitable habitat nearby and are increasingly numerous. The park is also home to lots of birds, from bald eagles, egrets, tundra swans, and herons to species uncommon across the rest of the state, like yellow-bellied sapsucker and hairy woodpecker.

13 Berlin Lake Mill Creek Recreation Area Campground

Location: West of Deerfield
Season: Late May–Sept.
Sites: 347, some ADA accessible
Maximum RV length: 82 feet
Facilities: Flush toilets, warm showers, sanitary dump station, water, electricity, picnic tables, playgrounds, volleyball courts, fire rings, environmental education programs, boat launch
Fee per night: $$$ to $$$$
Pets: Leashed pets permitted
Activities: Boating, hiking, fishing, hunting, waterskiing, tubing
Management: US Army Corps of Engineers, Pittsburgh District
Contact: (330) 547-3801; www.lrp.usace.army.mil/rec/lakes/berlin.htm. Reservations can be made through the National Recreation Reservation Service (NRRS) by calling toll free (877) 444-6777 or visiting www.Recreation.gov. There are some first come, first served campsites.
Finding the campground: From Deerfield, head east on US 224 for 3.7 miles. Turn right onto Beddell Road, go 0.9 mile, and look for the entrance to the campground on the right.
GPS coordinates: N 41 00.619' / W 80 59.241'
Other: This park has a group tenting site. Alcoholic beverages are prohibited.
About the campground: This is the largest campground operated by the Pittsburgh District of the Army Corps of Engineers. The park straddles the Pennsylvania-Ohio border—the campground is actually in Pennsylvania—and offers a good mix of shady, wooded sites and open sunny sites. There is a boat launching ramp within the campground that is free to campers.
Why it's worth a visit: There's probably no fish that tastes better than the walleye, and there are few inland waters better at producing them than Berlin Lake. It's known for its excellent fishing. Walleyes reproduce well enough here that the fishery does not need to be sustained through stocking, so you know it's good. Access to the lake is pretty nice, as well. The lake covers 3,950

acres, providing lots of room for boaters to roam, and offers 70 miles of shoreline. Much of it is gently to moderately sloped, so shore-bound anglers can enjoy some easy access. You've got a good chance to catch species other than walleyes, too. Largemouth and smallmouth bass, muskies, crappies and bluegills are all common. If you're looking for something to do other than fish, the woods surrounding the lake are a mix of beech and maples, which means there's some colorful foliage to see in the fall. Throughout the year birders can look for nesting ospreys and the occasional bald eagle. Hunters can pursue deer and small game, like squirrels, rabbits, and upland birds on the more than 6,800 acres managed for wildlife.

14 Beaver Creek State Park

Location: South of Youngstown
Season: Mar–Dec
Sites: 109, 59 for equestrians only
Maximum RV length: 25 feet
Facilities: Vault toilets, electricity, sanitary dump station, sun shower, water, picnic tables, fire rings, wildlife education center, pioneer village that hosts an annual fall festival, environmental education programs, playgrounds, boat launch, archery range
Fee per night: $$$$
Pets: Permitted at some sites
Activities: Boating, fishing, swimming, hiking, mountain biking, horseback riding, shooting, hunting
Management: Ohio Department of Natural Resources
Contact: (330) 385-3091; www.dnr.state.oh.us/parks/parks/beaverck/tabid/714/Default.aspx. For reservations call (866) 644-6727 or visit www.ohio.reserveworld.com. Equestrian sites are first come, first served.
Finding the campground: From Youngstown, follow I-680 south for about 7 miles. Take exit 14 onto SR 164 south/west for 3.3 miles, then a slight left onto Market Street/SR 7. Go 11.7 miles, stay straight to go onto Spruceville Road for 3.1 miles, then turn right onto Echo Dell Road. Go 1.5 miles to the park.
GPS coordinates: N 40 43.864' / W 80 37.138' for the family camp; N 40 42.750' / W 80 34.880' for the equestrian camp
Other: This park also has a primitive group camp and two teepees.
About the campground: The family campground is V-shaped with matching lollipops at the ends. Sites 43 to 50 offer the most privacy.
Why it's worth a visit: There's a lot to recommend this park in the foothills of the Appalachian Mountains, with hiking and biking trails, an archery range, pioneer village, old canal locks, and more spread across its more than 2,700 acres of forest wilderness. But three things really stand out. One is the paddling on the Little Beaver Creek, a national- and state-recognized Wild and Scenic River. It features water fast enough to be fun and some outstanding scenery while cutting through a gorge with high cliffs. Another is the Beaver Creek Wildlife Education Center. It's home to full body and head mounts of various mammals, wings, skulls, a live honey bee display, and more. You can explore it on your own—for free, no less—or take part in one of the many "explore the outdoors" programs offered throughout the year. A schedule and more information

A pair of horseback riders stop to let their mounts drink in Little Beaver Creek in Beaver Creek State Park.

are available at www.beavercreekwildlife.org/. Finally, this park is unique for its emphasis on bridle trails. There are 23 miles for horseback riders to explore.

15 Guilford Lake State Park

Location: West of Lisbon
Season: Year-round
Sites: 41, some walk-in only
Maximum RV length: 40 feet
Facilities: Flush toilets, warm showers, electricity, sanitary dump station, water, picnic tables, fire rings, water, playground, fishing dock, playground, basketball court, boat rental, boat launch, sports equipment available for loan
Fee per night: $$$$
Pets: Permitted at all sites
Activities: Swimming, boating, hiking, fishing, hunting
Management: Ohio Department of Natural Resources
Contact: (330) 222-1712; www.dnr.state.oh.us/parks/parks/guilford/tabid/739/Default.aspx. For reservations call (866) 644-6727 or visit www.ohio.reserveworld.com.
Finding the campground: From Lisbon, go west on US 30 for 2 miles. Take a slight right onto SR 172, go 3.9 miles and make a sharp right onto Baker Road. Go 0.2 mile, then take the first left

onto East Lake Road. Follow it until you can take a left onto Teegarden Road. Turn left just before crossing the lake, at the signs, and follow them to the campground.

GPS coordinates: N 40 48.402' / W 80 52.670'

Other: Though the campground is open year-round, certain facilities, like the shower house, are closed for portions of the year.

About the campground: This is a very spacious campground, with lots of room between sites. Some, like sites 7 and 8, are right on the lake, while others, like 36 and 28, are the most private.

Why it's worth a visit: This park has an interesting history, mostly centered on its 396-acre lake. Geologists believe Guilford Lake began as the result of a glacier that settled into a natural depression in the landscape and melted. Over time, the depression shrank and slowly filled in, becoming a swampy bog. It came back to life as a man-made impoundment in 1834. Meant to serve as a feeder reservoir for a canal that was to stretch over 73 miles. When that project closed, the lake was drained and turned into farmland. In time, the state bought it and rebuilt the reservoir. Ultimately it became the centerpiece of the park. Today, visitors swim in the lake and fish it for bass, bluegills, crappies, and channel catfish. It's also a fun lake on which to boat. Craft are limited to 10 horsepower, so it's a fairly serene water, if still busy at peak times. People bring their own boats, while a concessionaire rents some on the south shore and the campground rents canoes and paddleboats on the north shore.

16 Fernwood State Forest Hidden Hollow Campground

Location: East of Bloomingdale
Season: Year-round
Sites: 22
Maximum RV length: N/A
Facilities: Vault toilets, picnic tables, fire rings
Fee per night: Free
Pets: Permitted at all sites
Activities: Hiking, hunting, shooting, fishing
Management: Ohio Department of Natural Resources
Contact: (740) 266-6021; http://ohiodnr.com/DNN/forests/fernwood/tabid/5152/Default .aspx. Reservations are not available; first come, first served.
Finding the campground: From Bloomingdale, head east on CR 26/Fernwood-Bloomingdale Road for about 3 miles. Turn left to remain on CR 26 at the junction with Smithfield Station-Weems Road, then turn left at the sign to enter Hidden Hollow Campground.
GPS coordinates: N 40 20.074' / W 80 45.862'
Other: When you arrive here, select a site. A forest ranger will collect fees and issue a permit.
About the campground: The availability of water at this campground is spotty. Bring what you need just to be safe.
Why it's worth a visit: Fernwood is a forest built with sportsmen in mind. It's not big, at just a hair over 3,000 acres split between three tracts. But fishermen can hit the many small ponds, all of which have been stocked with largemouth bass, bluegills, and channel catfish. Hunters can chase white-tailed deer and small game species such as squirrels and grouse. They can also work on their marksmanship at the forest's public shooting ranges. Located southwest of Hidden Hollow

Campground are separate ranges for pistol, rifle, and shotgun shooting. Shooters must provide their own targets—paper or clay pigeons only—and pick up their casings and other debris before leaving, but it's a unique opportunity, especially for public land. Just outside the campground is the state forest's land lab, used to promote "natural resource and environmental education." You can explore it. Hiking, meanwhile, is available on Fernwood's largest tract. There's a 3-mile trail that winds around a picnic area and to two scenic vistas.

17 Friendship Park

Location: East of Cadiz
Season: Apr 1–Oct 31
Sites: 14
Maximum RV length: 50 feet
Facilities: Vault toilets, electricity, sanitary dump station, water (though not Oct 31–Apr 1), picnic tables, fire rings
Fee per night: $$$
Pets: Leashed pets permitted
Activities: Fishing, boating, bird watching, hiking, mountain biking, horseback riding, hunting
Management: Jefferson County
Contact: Reservations can be made by calling (740) 733-7941; www.jeffersoncountyoh.com/CountyOffices/FriendshipParkMainPage.aspx.
Finding the campground: From Cadiz, follow US 22 east for 5.9 miles. Take the exit toward SR 151 East for Hopedale/Smithfield, go 0.3 mile, then turn right onto SR 151/Mill Street and go 0.2 mile. Turn right onto Mill Street, go 0.5 mile, then turn left onto SR 151 East/Hopedale-Smithfield Road and go 6 miles. Turn left to stay on SR 151, go 1.1 miles, then take the first left onto Bloomingdale/Smithfield Road and go 0.4 mile. Make a sharp right onto Friendship Park Road, go 0.6 mile and follow the signs to CAMPGROUND.
GPS coordinates: N 40 17.152' / W 80 46.710'
Other: Bow hunting for deer is permitted. Hunters must contact the park for a free permit and orientation.
About the campground: Weekly and seasonal rates are available for this campground, which has been undergoing some expansion. A camper capable of holding five people is available for rent on a nightly or weekly basis, too.
Why it's worth a visit: Friendship Park is fairly large as most county facilities go, encompassing 1,320 acres. There's an 89-acre lake here and fishing for catfish, largemouth bass, bluegills, carp and trout is popular. All anglers sixteen and older need to buy a fishing permit; the money raised by their sale goes to stocking more fish. All fish but carp need to be released alive immediately. There are five smaller lakes here worth exploring, as are the wetlands and undeveloped areas. The smaller ponds are full of frogs, waterbirds and other creatures, while the woods hold white-tailed deer. The park is also home to the Jefferson County Fair in Aug, a two-day wine festival in September, and a privately-operated Steel Valley Dragway, which holds races throughout summer. Be sure to check out Fort Friendship, too. It's a veterans memorial with some interesting monuments.

18 Leesville Southfork Campground

Location: East of New Philadelphia
Season: Apr 1–Oct 31
Sites: 75
Maximum RV length: 50 feet
Facilities: Vault toilets, marina and restaurant, boat launch, boat rental, docks, sanitary dump station, electricity, water, picnic tables, fire rings
Fee per night: $$$$
Pets: Leashed pets permitted
Activities: Fishing, boating, hiking, hunting
Management: Muskingum Watershed Conservancy District
Contact: For reservations call (330) 343-6780; www.mwcd.org/places/parks/atwood-lake-park.
Finding the campground: From New Philadelphia, head east on SR 39 for 11.9 miles. Turn right onto SR 212/South Sherrod Avenue, go 0.3 mile, then turn left to stay on SR 212 and go 2.1 miles. Turn left onto Deer Road Southwest, go 0.8 mile, then turn right onto Azalea Road Southwest and go 0.07 mile. Take the first left onto Deer Road Southwest. Go 1 mile to the marina entrance and campground.
GPS coordinates: N 40 27.908' / W 81 11.377'
Other: This facility is also known locally as Clow's Marina. It's managed by the staff at Atwood Lake Park.
About the campground: This campground offers nightly and seasonal camping and thirty-day stays. It's located on the lake's southern end. There's also a private marina and campground on the northern end of the lake, as well as a few rentable cabins.
Why it's worth a visit: This long, narrow, C-shaped lake, impounded in 1938, is a little bit of wilderness. That's because no roads encircle it. Instead, its 27 miles of pine tree-covered shoreline give the place a remote feel. Anglers enjoy it as it's considered an excellent fishery for largemouth bass and muskies and a good one for crappies, and bluegills. A 10-horsepower limit is in effect on the lake. A fishing map available from the state Department of Natural Resources (find it at www.dnr.state.oh.us/Portals/9/pdf/lakemaps/LeesvilleLake.pdf) offers details on lake contours, amenities and more. Hikers who explore the shorelines and the Leesville Lake Wildlife Area, which fills the "C" created by it, will find a variety of songbirds. Hunters can pursue white-tailed deer, as well as turkeys and grouse.

19 Atwood Lake Park

Location: South of Mineral City
Season: Year-round
Sites: 600
Maximum RV length: 35 feet, with some longer pull-through sites

Facilities: Flush toilets, warm showers, electricity, water, sanitary dump station, picnic tables, fire rings, playground, boat rentals, boat launch, activity and nature center, environmental education and other programming, laundry facility, camp store, free WiFi at the activity center
Fee per night: $$$$
Pets: Leashed pets permitted
Activities: Hiking, hunting, swimming, fishing, boating
Management: Muskingum Watershed Conservancy District
Contact: For reservations call (330) 343-6780; www.mwcd.org/places/parks/atwood-lake-park. Some sites are first come, first served during the off-season.
Finding the campground: From Mineral City, head southeast on CR 90/New Cumberland Road for 5.2 miles. Turn left onto CR 114/Lakeview Road and follow the signs for about 2 miles to the park entrance.
GPS coordinates: N 40 32.644' / W 81 16.127'
Other: Atwood hosts a Christian music festival every June and a fall festival every Oct. It also rents cabins and has an organized group camping area.
About the campground: The campground is broken down into several sections, each consisting of loops and all generally close to the lake. Seasonal passes good for seven months are available on a limited basis.
Why it's worth a visit: Atwood Lake Park is a big one at more than 3,000 acres. The lake itself adds another 1,500-plus acres and is the main attraction. It's a favorite with boaters—it's considered one of Ohio's premier sailing sites—and fishermen who pursue largemouth bass, channel catfish, crappies, bluegills, yellow perch, northern pike, and saugeyes. Two marinas cater to all those people. You can have your boat serviced, rent one by the hour or for the day, gas up, or even get a meal. There are a few small hiking trails here, too, along with a swimming beach. In general, this park—like all those run by the Watershed Conservancy—is similar to some private operations in that it's long on services. Here there are a good many regularly scheduled events, a game center and Internet access. It's a good place to introduce someone to camping without having to give up too many creature comforts.

20 Sally Buffalo Park

Location: Southwest of Cadiz
Season: Apr 1–Nov 1, though tent camping can be done year-round
Sites: 300
Maximum RV length: No restrictions
Facilities: Showers, flush toilets, electricity, water, sanitary dump stations, laundry, picnic tables, fire rings, playgrounds, basketball and tennis courts, horseshoe pits, concession stand
Fee per night: $$$ to $$$$
Pets: Leashed pets permitted
Activities: Hiking, fishing, boating, swimming, sports, biking
Management: Village of Cadiz
Contact: Reservations can be made by calling (740) 942-3213; http://pages.eohio.net/sallybuffalo/.

Finding the campground: From Cadiz, follow South Main Street/SR 9 for 0.2 mile, then turn right onto Grant Street and go 1.2 miles. Turn left onto Industrial Park Road and go 0.3 mile to the park entrance, then follow the signs to CAMPGROUND.

GPS coordinates: N 40 15.810' / W 81 01.077'

Other: This park also rents two vacation cabins.

About the campground: The campground consists of several loops. Some have limited availability. Seasonal passes are available to those who want to stay long-term.

Why it's worth a visit: Sally Buffalo? The unusual name of this park traces its roots to a former landowner and his wife. A Revolutionary War soldier from Pennsylvania, John McFadden, settled here, bringing with him a son named Samuel Buffalo McFadden. He married a woman named Sally and together they built a grist mill powered by the stream here. The mill and that water took the name of Sally Buffalo and it stuck. The mill ultimately went out of business, and that set in motion an interesting industrial history for this site. A century later, in 1953, Hanna Coal Co. built the first lake and park for employees. A dozen years later it was opened to the public. Five years after that new owner Consol Energy Co. took over. The land then changed hands several more times until 1990, when the Village of Cadiz finally took over. Today visitors can hike several miles of trail, including a 1-mile paved trail around the largest of the lake. There's also fishing in four man-made lakes; all can be tried without first having to buy a fishing license. An accessible dock on that lake is the result of one of the several Eagle Scout projects that have been completed here.

21 Harrison State Forest Trailriders and Ronsheim Campgrounds

Location: North of Cadiz

Season: Year-round

Sites: 27

Maximum RV length: N/A

Facilities: Vault toilets, picnic tables, fire rings, water, hitching posts

Fee per night: Free

Pets: Permitted at all sites

Activities: Horseback riding, hiking, hunting

Management: Ohio Department of Natural Resources

Contact: (740) 266-6021; http://ohiodnr.com/forestry/forests/harrison/tabid/5155/Default .aspx. Reservations are not available; it's first come, first served.

Finding the campgrounds: From Cadiz, head north on SR 9 for 2 miles. Turn right onto Township Road 185 to reach Trailriders Campground. Turn right onto CR 13, then left onto Township Road 189 to reach Ronsheim Campground.

GPS coordinates: N 40 20.355' / W 81 01.512' for Trailriders Campground; N 40 19.809' / W 80 59.377' for Ronsheim Campground

Other: When you arrive, simply pick an open site and a ranger will show up to give you a permit and go over the camp rules.

About the campground: There are seven family campsites at Ronsheim Campground, twenty accommodating family or horse campers at Trailriders Campground.

Why it's worth a visit: This 1,345-acre forest in Harrison County is a relatively new one, by public standards. It wasn't purchased until 1961. Of course, it wasn't much of a forest then either. The area had been heavily strip-mined, with just the steeper ridges and deeper valleys left untouched. The state purchased the area and planted more than 100,000 trees. That—combined with the fact acid mine water is not much of a problem, given the presence of so much limestone in the ground—has made this a wooded wonderland of sorts. There are not a lot of modern amenities on hand. Solitude is the most common thing. But there are 24 miles of trails, suitable for horseback riders or hikers. They lead past mature and developing forests, roads, and ponds, some of them good for fishing for warmwater species like bass and bluegills. Wildlife like deer, squirrels, turkeys, raccoons, and songbirds are plentiful. Hunters enjoy this area not only because of the wildlife. There's also a 100-yard public shooting range where people can shoot for fun or sight in their firearms. You've got to obey the posted rules and share it with others, but it's a fun—and free—option.

22 Tappan Lake Park

Location: Southeast of Uhrichsville
Season: Year-round
Sites: 500
Maximum RV length: 35 feet, with some longer pull-through sites
Facilities: Flush toilets, warm showers, electricity, water, sanitary dump station, picnic tables, fire rings, playground, nature and activity centers, environmental education and other programming, laundry facilities, camp store, boat launch, amphitheater
Fee per night: $$$$
Pets: Leashed pets permitted
Activities: Hunting, swimming, waterskiing, fishing, boating, hiking
Management: Muskingum Watershed Conservancy District
Contact: For reservations call (740) 922-3649; www.mwcd.org/places/parks/tappan-lake-park. Some sites are first come, first served during the off-season.
Finding the campground: From Uhrichsville, head east on US 250 for 15.5 miles. Turn right onto Deersville Road, go 1.8 miles, then continue another 1.9 miles after it becomes Deersville Ridge Road. Turn right onto Tappan Lake Park Road and follow it to the entrance to the park and the campground.
GPS coordinates: N 40 18.694' / W 81 10.900'
Other: This park also rents camper cabins and vacation cabins.
About the campground: The campground has one entrance, but is broken into two sections, one for tents and one that also allows RVs.
Why it's worth a visit: All of the Watershed Conservancy's lands surround large lakes, and Tappen Lake Park is no exception. It's home to a 2,350-acre lake surrounded by 5,000 acres of woodlands. That means it's got waterskiing and tubing, though you should be sure to follow the recommended guidelines regarding which direction to travel. There are quieter bays for picnicking and fishing for channel and flathead catfish, white bass, largemouth bass, crappies, yellow perch, walleyes, saugeyes, and bluegills. There's swimming at a beach. But this park is a gem for hikers,

too. It's got more than the usual fishermen's paths around the water's edge. The North Country and Buckeye trails pass through the park. Another trail leads from the campground to the Tappan Wetlands, a designated watchable wildlife area. There you can often see birds like great blue herons, muskrats, frogs, and more. Other trails—some as long as 6 miles—explore the area between the campground and Bontrager Bay. If you want to get really adventurous, the trails can be combined to create an all-day excursion.

23 Tuscarawas County Fairgrounds

Location: South of Massillon
Season: Apr–Oct
Sites: 200
Maximum RV length: No limit
Facilities: Showers, flush toilets, electricity, sanitary dump station, water
Fee per night: $$ to $$$
Pets: Leashed pets permitted
Activities: Hiking, fishing, playgrounds, attractions all nearby
Management: Tuscarawas County Agricultural Society
Contact: For reservations call (330) 343-0524; www.tuscarawascountyfair.com/.
Finding the campground: From Massillon, head south on SR 21 for 11.4 miles. Continue straight for another 3 miles after SR 21 becomes US 250. Merge onto I-77 south and go 4.2 miles, then take exit 83 toward Sugarcreek/Dover. Go 0.2 mile, then turn left onto SR 39/Tuscarawas Avenue and go 1.6 miles to the fairground entrance. Follow signs to FAIR OFFICE.
GPS coordinates: N 40 30.894' / W 81 28.347'
Other: Weekly and seasonal rates are available. There's a waiting list for camp space during the annual fair, held in September.
About the campground: Most of the campsites are along what serves as the midway during fair week. They are mostly in sun, with some trees nearby.
Why it's worth a visit: This fairgrounds is the staging ground for a lot of activities. People with relatives in the area come here to stay, as do concessionaires working festivals throughout the region. You can turn it into the base for a pretty neat vacation, too. Dover City Park is very close by and offers everything from a swimming pool and basketball courts to baseball fields and a professional-grade disc golf course. Also in the immediate area is the Norma Johnson Conservation Center. Operated by the Tuscarawas Soil and Water Conservation District, it's a 303-acre reserve with miles of marked trails. They take you past wetlands, bluebird nest boxes, and five ponds, and over suspension and footbridges. Open from dawn to dusk year-round, it's a great place to do some birding or otherwise watch wildlife. Details and direction can be found at www .normajohnsoncenter.com. There's also paddling and fishing on the Tuscarawas River, which flows right past the fairgrounds. Several liveries operate in the area if you need to rent equipment. The local convention and visitors bureau (http://traveltusc.com/) has details.

24 Coshocton Lake Park

Location: East of Randle
Season: Apr 1–Dec. 15
Sites: 69
Maximum RV length: 40 feet
Facilities: Flush toilets, showerhouse, electricity, water, sanitary dump station, picnic tables, fire rings, water, playground, small camp store at the office, ballfields, pool
Fee per night: $$$$
Pets: Leashed pets permitted
Activities: Road and mountain biking, hiking, golfing, swimming, canal boat rides
Management: Coshocton County
Contact: For reservations call (740) 622-7528; www.coshoctonlakepark.com/index.htm.
Finding the campground: From Randle, head east on US 36 for 4.2 miles. Turn left onto US 36/SR 83 and go 0.3 mile, then turn left again onto SR 83 and go 0.5 mile. Turn left into the park and follow the signs for CAMPGROUND.
GPS coordinates: N 40 17.429' / W 81 52.334'
Other: The maximum length of stay is fourteen consecutive days. Alcoholic beverages are prohibited in the park.
About the campground: All campers must register at the office or with a ranger upon arrival.
Why it's worth a visit: Coshocton Lake Park seems equal parts historic site, amusement park, and nature reserve. The historical part of the equation is the horse-drawn canal boat rides offered in a restored 1.5-mile section of the Ohio-Erie Canal. The *Monticello III* operates afternoons Tuesday–Sunday from Memorial Day through Labor Day. There's a fee to ride, but it's a neat experience. The amusement park comes in two forms: an 18-hole golf course that will appeal to adults and an aquatic center for young and old. It's an impressive facility for a county park, with twisting water slides, fountains and a playground inside the pool. Entry requires paying a daily or seasonal fee. When it comes to exploring nature, Coshocton Lake Park has several trails of note. The Three Rivers Bikeway is a paved path that is supposed to eventually connect the park to the town of Coshocton; bike rentals are available. The Towpath is a paved hike and bike trail that follows the path of the original Ohio-Erie Canal and crosses the Walhonding River via a rebuilt aqueduct footbridge. Finally, the park's newest trail is the Eagle Ridge Trail. It connects with others to create a 7.5-mile system of trails that parallel the river, pass scenic sandstone ledges, and wind through forest.

25 Mohican State Park

Location: South of Ashland
Season: Apr–Dec
Sites: 186
Maximum RV length: 50 feet
Facilities: Flush toilets, electricity, warm showers, sanitary dump station, water, picnic tables, fire rings, camp store, swimming pool, volleyball and basketball courts, sports equipment available for loan, environmental education programming, Wolf Creek/Pine Run Grist Mill Museum

A covered bridge crosses the Clear Fork of the Mohican River in Mohican State Park, Hemlock Grove.

Fee per night: $$$$
Pets: Permitted at all sites
Activities: Hiking, biking, horseback riding, boating, fishing, hunting
Management: Ohio Department of Natural Resources
Contact: (419) 994-5125; www.dnr.state.oh.us/parks/parks/mohican/tabid/769/Default.aspx. For reservations call (866) 644-6727 or visit www.ohio.reserveworld.com.
Finding the campground: From Ashland, head south on SR 60/511 for 17.8 miles. Turn right onto East Main Street/SR 39, go 0.2 mile, then take the third left onto South Market Street/SR 3. Follow the signs to CAMPGROUND.
GPS coordinates: N 40 36.577' / W 82 15.466'
Other: This park rents camping cottages and cabins and has a group camping area and lodge and conference center. There's a small, nine-site Class B camping area—Hemlock Grove—with self-registration near the covered bridge across Clear Fork of the Mohican River.
About the campground: This is a large campground built on an industrial scale in the sense that it's got a lot of sites crammed together. There are pull-through pads on odd-numbered sites in parts of the campground.
Why it's worth a visit: The Clear Fork of Mohican River, which flows through the park, is one of the finest canoeing rivers in Ohio. What makes it special is the gorge through which it passes. A registered National Natural Landmark, it's more than 300 feet deep and more than 1,000 feet wide at the top, with exposed sandstone rock walls, towering hemlocks, and stands of ancient white pine to be seen along the way. There's some outstanding fishing to be had, too. The river is stocked with brown trout. Bass, crappies, bluegills, saugers, and even the occasional musky swim here, too.

There are no liveries within the park, but you can rent boats from several sources nearby or bring your own. Campers have access to two canoe and inner-tube launches. They start on the west end of the campground, with a take-out at the east end. There are also some wonderful trails in this park. The North Rim, Hemlock, and Song Bird Trails all start or run through the campground. You can ride 25 miles of bike trail or cover other miles on your horse.

26 Mohican-Memorial State Forest Park and Pack Camp

Location: East of Butler
Season: Year-round
Sites: 10
Maximum RV length: N/A
Facilities: Vault toilets, picnic tables, fire rings, water, hitching posts
Fee per night: Free
Pets: Permitted at all sites
Activities: Horseback riding, hiking, hunting, mountain biking, snowmobiling, cross-country skiing
Management: Ohio Department of Natural Resources
Contact: (419) 938-6222; http://ohiodnr.com/forestry/forests/mohican/tabid/5160/Default
.aspx. Reservations are not available; it's first come, first served.
Finding the campground: To reach the Mohican State Park office, which serves as an entry point to the forest and the scattered park and pack sites, head east on SR 97 for 9.5 miles. Turn left onto SR 3 and go 0.3 mile to the forest office, then follow signs to CAMPING AREA.
GPS coordinates: N 40 36.583' / W 82 15.469'
Other: This forest receive thousands of visitors annually. Be sure to pack out all that you pack in to keep it clean and wild.
About the campground: The sites here are considered "park and pack" ones, meaning you have to leave your vehicle and carry your gear. It's not backpacking, but the sites aren't at the edge of the parking lot either.
Why it's worth a visit: There's simply a lot to do at Mohican-Memorial State Forest, at all times of year. There are 32 miles of trails for hikers and 22 more open to both hikers and horseback riders. Cross-country skiers use some of those in winter, while snowmobilers have a designated 8-mile route that doubles as a mountain biking path. Cyclists have another option in the form of a 24-mile loop with two trailheads built and maintained by volunteers. Some specific sites beckon visitors. The Memorial Shrine is a section of forest—complete with a sandstone chapel—set aside to honor war veterans, while Pine Run Creek is very picturesque. Clear Fork Gorge State Nature Preserve, a 29-acre tract overlooking the officially designated wild and scenic Mohican River, is home to rare nesting warblers, round-leaver orchids and some of the oldest hemlocks in the state. You can also get some very nice views by visiting the fire tower. And, if you pay attention, you can see some work of Civilian Conservation Corps workers in the 1930s. Then, young men were paid to reforest old, abandoned farmsteads. The job was meant to provide income during the Great Depression while rebuilding landscapes at the same time. Some of the red and white pine planta-tions created by those crews are still visible.

An overlook in Mohican-Memorial State Forest offers a panoramic view.

27 Pleasant Hill Lake Park

Location: West of Perrysville
Season: Year-round
Sites: 417
Maximum RV length: 35 feet, with some longer pull-through sites
Facilities: Flush toilets, warm showers, electricity, water, sanitary dump station, picnic tables, fire rings, playground, boat rentals, boat launch, environmental education and other programming, basketball and volleyball courts, camp store, free WiFi available at the activity center
Fee per night: $$$$
Pets: Leashed pets permitted
Activities: Hiking, hunting, swimming, waterskiing, fishing, horseback riding, boating
Management: Muskingum Watershed Conservancy District
Contact: For reservations call (419) 938-7884; www.mwcd.org/places/parks/pleasant-hill-lake-park. Some sites are first come, first served during the off-season.
Finding the campground: From downtown Perrysville, go north on SR 39 for about a half mile. Turn left onto SR 95 and go 1.6 miles, then turn left to enter the park. The two sections of the campground split at the next Y.
GPS coordinates: N 40 39.102' / W 82 20.436'
Other: This park has a group camping area and rents camper cabins, patio cabins, and a house. It also rents thirty-seven camp sites designed specifically for people with horses.

About the campground: The campground consists of five separate loops, with A through D in one area and E in another. The horse camp is located in between the two.

Why it's worth a visit: Pleasant Hill has one of the smaller lakes operated by the Muskingum Watershed Conservancy at 850 acres. But it allows boaters to operate with unlimited horsepower, which makes this a favorite place for those who like to water ski and tube. You can balance your need for speed with some quiet time, though. The western third of the lake is managed as a no-wake zone. One of the lake's two areas where boaters can swim off their craft is there. That area is also popular with fishermen, who pursue muskies, channel catfish, largemouth, smallmouth and white bass, crappies, bluegills, yellow perch, and saugeyes. Away from the water, the park takes in more than 1,300 acres. A new and developing system of bridle trails winds through those woods and fields and is attracting some attention. Hikers make use of those same pathways. This park is also located adjacent to Malabar Farm State Park and Mohican State Forest, so you can camp here and explore those other places in day trips.

28 Charles Mill Lake Park

Location: East of Mansfield
Season: Year-round
Sites: 500
Maximum RV length: 35 feet, with some longer pull-through sites
Facilities: Flush toilets, warm showers, electricity, water, sanitary dump station, picnic tables, fire rings, playground, boat rentals, boat launch, environmental education and other programming, basketball, volleyball, shuffleboard and bocce ball courts, disc golf course, camp store, free WiFi at the activity center
Fee per night: $$$$
Pets: Leashed pets permitted
Activities: Disc golf, swimming, fishing, boating, hiking, hunting
Management: Muskingum Watershed Conservancy District
Contact: For reservations call (419) 368-6885; www.mwcd.org/places/parks/charles-mill-lake -park. Some sites are first come, first served during the off-season.
Finding the campground: From Mansfield, head east on SR 430 for about 7 miles. The entrance to the campground will be on the left.
GPS coordinates: N 40 46.197' / W 82 22.755'
Other: This park also rents patio and camper cabins.
About the campground: The campground is broken into two pieces. Eagle Point is by itself, away from most of the day-use sites. Additional camping is offered closer to the park entrance and Fisherman's Point.
Why it's worth a visit: Charles Mill Lake, built in 1935, takes in 1,350 acres and offers 34 miles of shoreline. It's surrounded by 2,000 acres of woods and fields. That means there are plenty of nature-based things to keep you busy. There's fishing for channel and flathead catfish, largemouth bass, white bass, hybrid striped bass—called wipers who offer powerful, bulldog-like fights when hooked—crappies, bluegills, and saugeyes. There is some hiking as well, and opportunities to hunt deer, turkeys, and small game. You can swim and visit playgrounds, too. But if you want to socialize, this park offers all kinds of opportunities to do that, courtesy of the many special events it

A flock of geese wing their way across the sky near the dam at Charles Mill Lake Park.

hosts throughout the year. In May–Oct there are Mother's Day breakfasts and crafts, ice-cream weekends, fireworks, dog-friendly events, pig roasts, carnivals, chili cook-offs, and more. That's partly a reflection of the number of people who set up camp here for the summer, but all are welcome to get involved. If you like making friends, this may be the place for you.

29 Malabar Farm State Park

Location: Southeast of Mansfield
Season: Early Apr–late Nov
Sites: 15
Maximum RV length: 50 feet
Facilities: Vault toilets, water, picnic tables, fire rings, restaurant
Fee per night: $$$ to $$$$
Pets: Permitted at all sites
Activities: Hiking, fishing, tours of the Louis Bromfield Mansion, wagon tours of the farm
Management: Ohio Department of Natural Resources
Contact: (419) 892-2784; www.dnr.state.oh.us/parks/parks/malabar/tabid/762/Default.aspx. For reservations call (866) 644-6727 or visit www.ohio.reserveworld.com.
Finding the campground: From Mansfield, head east on SR 430 until you can turn right/south onto Lucas Road/SR 39. Go 5.3 miles, then turn right onto South Union Street and go 0.1 mile.

Take a slight left onto Railroad Street, go 0.1 mile, then continue 2.7 miles as Railroad Street becomes Moffet Street. Turn left onto Pleasant Valley Road, go 1.4 miles, and turn onto Bromfield Road and go 0.4 mile.

GPS coordinates: N 40 39.103' / W 82 23.626'

Other: This park is also home to a nineteen-room hostel. A 1919 mail-order catalog house, it's where Louis Bromfield and his family lived while their mansion was being built. Call (419) 892-2055 for reservations. There's also an equestrian campground here.

About the campground: This is a small campground, with all of the sites opposite one another, like the veins on a leaf. That lends itself to lots of privacy and a nice facility.

Why it's worth a visit: This is one of the most interesting and unusual state parks you will ever come across. You can do the usual stuff here, like hike, fish, and swim. But this is also a working farm. It was created by Pulitzer Prize–winning author Louis Bromfield in the first half of the twentieth century and, after his death and as was his wish, became a state park in 1976. Today, visitors can explore that history firsthand. The farm still raises chickens, goats, and beef cattle. You can enjoy some of the benefits of the farm—the roadside stand that's been in operation since 1952 still sells produce from Memorial Day weekend through Oct—by taking guided wagon tours of the farm and its gardens or visiting the petting barn. There's also the Malabar Inn. It's a restored 1820 stagecoach inn located within the park's boundaries. It's open Tuesday through Sunday year-round and offers home-cooked meals using the fruits of the farm. Bromfield's thirty-two-room mansion, the "Big House," is open for guided tours, too. And while you are here, be sure to check out the Mt. Jeez Scenic Overlook. It's the panoramic overlook where Bromfield used to take visitors while he described the operations of his farm.

30 Findley State Park

Location: South of Wellington
Season: Year-round
Sites: 271
Maximum RV length: 50 feet
Facilities: Flush toilets, warm showers, electricity, laundry facilities, sanitary dump station, water, picnic tables, fire rings, camp store, playground, volleyball and basketball courts, nature center, environmental education programs, boat launches, disc golf course
Fee per night: $$$$
Pets: Permitted at all sites
Activities: Boating, hiking, mountain biking, swimming, disc golf, hunting, fishing
Management: Ohio Department of Natural Resources
Contact: (440) 647-5749; www.dnr.state.oh.us/parks/parks/findley/tabid/734/Default.aspx. For reservations call (866) 644-6727 or visit www.ohio.reserveworld.com.
Finding the campground: From Wellington, head due south on SR 58 for 2.5 miles to the park, then follow the signs to CAMPGROUND.
GPS coordinates: N 41 07.444' / W 82 12.367'
Other: While here, visit nearby Wellington. About 75 percent of its downtown is on the National Register of Historic Places.

Cows graze at the base of the Mt. Jeez overlook in Malabar Farm State Park.

About the campground: There are two organized group camping areas here, along with three "Conestoga" camper cabins that are available Apr–Oct.

Why it's worth a visit: This is farm country famous for its dairy industry: It once produced as much cheese as any place in the nation. The park is a different sort of beast, however. Its 838 acres were once a state forest, as is evidenced by its vast hardwoods and pines. There are some interesting wooded paths to walk. There are 16 miles of trail open to hiking and biking, as well as a 9-mile loop trail for bikers. It features short steep climbs, fast winding sections, bank turns, and north shore obstacles to challenge riders of all levels. One of the park's main attractions is its 93-acre lake. Fishermen like it because it's full of largemouth bass, bluegills, and crappies, while boaters—especially those with canoes and kayaks—like it because it's open only to unpowered boats and those with electric motors. Paddle around on misty mornings and you can often see some interesting wildlife, from turtles to waterbirds. The park hosts nature programs, too.

Southeast

Remember that old Sesame Street children's song, the one that said "one of these things is not like the other?" That's southeastern Ohio.

There are parks here that have big lakes, as in other parts of the state. Salt Fork State Park's lake in particular is more than 2,000 acres. There are a couple of county fairgrounds that offer camping, as elsewhere. There are hiking trails and bridle trails and fishing, as elsewhere.

But the topography here is so different that this region feels more like neighboring West Virginia that the rest of Ohio. If you want to talk about any part of the state being wild, this is it. It's home to the some of the largest chunks of public land to be found anywhere in the state, some of them with the fewest amenities.

You can experience that in a couple of ways.

Hocking Hills State Park—rated by one website as having the best campground in the nation—showcases the oddities of the terrain in this part of Ohio. It's cut by gorges and pockmarked with caves and caverns. Some of those caverns are so large they look almost unnatural; you could imagine them as movie sets, with scenes of desperados making their last stand. The fact that real-life hermits lived out their days here only adds to the mystique.

This region is also home to Ohio's only national forest, the Wayne. It takes in nearly a quarter-million acres. It's an interesting place. Broken into chunks, with a fair bit of active timber management and gas drilling within it, the Wayne doesn't always feel like wilderness. But it does feel big. It's got a good number of campgrounds and also allows dispersed camping, where you park at a trailhead or wide spot in the road and set up camp. There's nowhere else in the state where you can do that.

This is also the one place in Ohio where you can camp along a scenic byway marked by old-time covered bridges.

There's a lot of history in this area as well. Zanesville was the boyhood home of Zane Gray, the prolific writer of Western novels and adventurous fishing tales, and there's a museum dedicated to his life. Hopalong Cassidy and Clark Gable have museums, too. There's even one centered on the Bob Evans restaurant chain.

What all that means is, if you want to go primitive, this is the place to do it. But when you're ready to come out of the woods—ending your own hermit-like existence for a while—there will be plenty of attractions awaiting you.

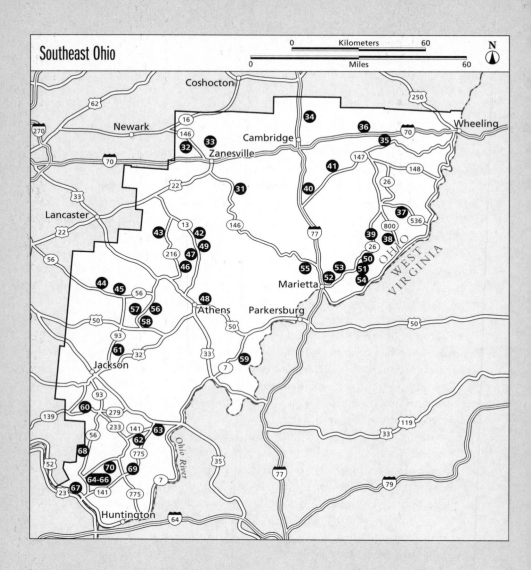

Southeast Ohio

Wild and Wonderful Ohio

	total sites	hookups	max RV lengths	toilets	showers	drinking water	dump station	recreation	fee	reservation
31 Blue Rock State Park	97	N	50	V	Y	Y	Y	HBFSRLU	$$$	Y
32 Dillon State Park	195	Y	50	F	Y	Y	Y	HBFSCLU	$$$$	Y
33 Muskingum River Parkway State Park	20	N	30	V	N	Y	N	BF	$$$	Y
34 Salt Fork State Park	192	Y	50	F	Y	Y	Y	HBFSLUEE	$$$$	Y
35 Barkcamp State Park	152	Y	35	F	Y	Y	Y	HBFSLRUEE	$$$$	Y
36 Piedmont Marina Campground	80	Y	35	F	Y	Y	Y	FB	$$$$	Y
37 Piatt Park	11	Y	30	F	Y	Y	N	H	$$$	Y
38 Ring Mill Campground	3	N	N/A	V	N	N	N	HBF	N/A	N
39 Lamping Homestead	6	N	N/A	V	N	N	N	HBFCU	N/A	Y
40 Wolf Run State Park	138	Y	50	F	Y	Y	Y	HBFSLU	$$$$	Y
41 Seneca Lake Park	513	Y	35	F	Y	Y	Y	HBFSLEEU	$$$$	Y
42 Wildcat Hollow	N/A	N	N/A	V	N	N	N	H	N/A	N
43 Stone Church Horse Camp	10	N	45	V	N	N	N	HRU	$$	N
44 Hocking Hills State Park	169	Y	50	F	Y	Y	Y	HFSCU	$$$$	Y
45 Hocking State Forest Horse Camp	23	N	N/A	V	N	Y	N	HRU	N/A	N
46 Monday Creek	N/A	N	N/A	V	N	N	N	HCUO	N/A	N
47 Burr Oak State Park	95	Y	40	F	Y	Y	Y	HBFSLRU	$$$$	Y
48 Strouds Run State Park	78	N	40	V	N	N	N	HBFSLRU	$$$-$$$$	N
49 Burr Oak Cove Campground	19	N	45	V	N	Y	N	HFU	$$$	N
50 Haught Run Campground	4	N	45	V	N	N	N	HBF	N/A	N
51 Hune Bridge Campground	3	N	N/A	V	N	N	N	HBF	N/A	N
52 Lane Farm Campground	4	N	40	V	N	N	N	F	N/A	N
53 Leith Run Recreation Area	21	Y	90	F	Y	Y	Y	HBF	$$$-$$$$	Y
54 Kinderhook Horse Trail	N/A	N	N/A	V	N	N	N	HRU	N/A	N
55 Washington County Fairgrounds	100	Y	N/A	F	Y	Y	Y	HBFC	$$$-$$$$	N
56 Lake Hope State Park	187	Y	50	V	Y	Y	Y	HBFSCLRUEE	$$$$	Y
57 Zaleski State Forest	16	N	N/A	V	N	Y	N	HRU	N/A	N
58 Vinton Furnace State Experimental Forest	3	N	N/A	V	N	N	N	HFU	N/A	N

59 Forked Run State Park	146	Y	50	V	Y	Y	Y	HBFSCLU	$$$$	Y
60 Jackson Lake State Park	34	Y	50	V	N	Y	Y	BFSLEEU	$$$$	Y
61 Lake Alma State Park	81	Y	50	V	N	Y	Y	HBFSCL	$$$$	Y
62 Raccoon Creek Park	6	N	N/A	V	N	Y	N	HFB	$$$$	Y
63 Gallia County Fairgrounds	200	Y	50	F	Y	Y	Y	N/A	$$$$	Y
64 Lake Vesuvius Iron Ridge Campground	41	Y	45	V	N	Y	Y	HBFRU	$$$	Y
65 Lake Vesuvius Oak Hill Campground	28	Y	45	F	Y	Y	Y	HBFSRU	$$$$	Y
66 Lake Vesuvius Pine Knob Campground	16	N	N/A	V	N	Y	N	HBFSRU	$$$	N
67 Hanging Rock Trail System	N/A	N	N/A	V	N	N	N	HBFCOU	N/A	N
68 Pine Creek Trail System	N/A	N	N/A	V	N	N	N	HCUO	N/A	N
69 Timbre Ridge Lake	N/A	N	N/A	V	N	N	N	HBFSLU	N/A	N
70 Vesuvius Horse Trail	N/A	N	N/A	V	N	N	N	HRU	N/A	N

See fee codes on page xx and amenities codes on page xxiii.

31 Blue Rock State Park

Location: South of Zanesville
Season: Year-round, though the non-electric sites are closed from Jan–Mar
Sites: 97, some walk-in only
Maximum RV length: 50 feet
Facilities: Vault toilets, warm showers at the beach house, water, picnic tables, fire rings, sanitary dump station, volleyball and basketball courts, boat launch, horseshoe pits, playground, seasonal camp store
Fee per night: $$$
Pets: Permitted at some sites
Activities: Horseback riding, boating, fishing, hiking, swimming, hunting
Management: Ohio Department of Natural Resources
Contact: (740) 453-4377; www.dnr.state.oh.us/parks/parks/bluerock/tabid/715/Default.aspx. For reservations call (866) 644-6727 or visit www.ohio.reserveworld.com.
Finding the campground: From Zanesville, go south on SR 60/River Road for 9.1 miles until you can turn left onto Cutler Lake Road. Go 0.5 mile, turn right to stay on Cutler Lake Road, go 0.2 mile, then take the first right to stay on Cutler Lake Road. Go 1.3 miles. At the Y, turn right to stay on Cutler Lake Road and follow it 3.5 miles into the park. The campground entrance will be on your right.
GPS coordinates: N 39 49.116' / W 81 51.098'
Other: This park has three rent-a-camp units, three camper cabins and an organized group tenting area.
About the campground: Some of the walk-in only sites here are really nice. Sites 20 to 24 are closest to the lake, while 51 to 56 are closest to the playground.

50 Haught Run Campground

Location: Northeast of Marietta
Season: Year-round
Sites: 4
Maximum RV length: 45 feet
Facilities: Vault toilets, picnic tables, fire rings
Fee per night: Free
Pets: Leashed pets permitted
Activities: Fishing, paddling, hiking, backpacking, wildlife watching
Management: Wayne National Forest
Contact: (740) 373-9055; www.fs.usda.gov/wayne. No reservations are taken; it's first come, first served.
Finding the campground: From Marietta, follow SR 26 northeast for about 20 miles. The campground will be on the right, shortly after you pass through the town of Wingett Run.
GPS coordinates: N 39 32.039' / W 81 13.413'
Other: This campground does not offer water, so bring your own.
About the campground: Despite its beauty, this campground does not attract an awful lot of overnight guests, so chances of getting one of its few spaces are generally pretty good, especially on weekdays.
Why it's worth a visit: Haught Run is another of the four campgrounds that exist along the Covered Bridge Scenic Byway and the Muskingum River. There are a couple of ways to see it. In spring, early summer or whenever there's enough water in the river, you can paddle this. The water will be brown; Muskingum is a Native American word for "muddy river," after all. But it's a nice float—considered southeast Ohio's best, in fact—that will take you past historic barns, century-old farmhouses, covered bridges, rocky bluffs and some picturesque farmland scenery. Bring your fishing rod and camera. Anglers who cast into the Muskingum can find smallmouth bass, panfish, and muskies, while wildlife watchers can expect to see animals typical of a lowland hardwood forest, like white-tailed deer, raccoons, muskrats, frogs, herons, and more. When the water's too low to canoe or kayak, or when you just prefer traveling by foot, you can hike. An 8-mile trail links the Hune and Rinard covered bridges. Another connector will put you on the North Country National Scenic Trail.

51 Hune Bridge Campground

Location: Northeast of Marietta
Season: Year-round
Sites: 3
Maximum RV length: N/A
Facilities: Vault toilets, picnic tables, fire rings, interpretive signage
Fee per night: Free
Pets: Leashed pets permitted
Activities: Fishing, paddling, hiking, backpacking

Management: Wayne National Forest
Contact: (740) 373-9055; www.fs.usda.gov/wayne. No reservations are taken; it's first come, first served.
Finding the campground: From Marietta, follow SR 26 northeast for about 12 miles. The campground will be on the right, shortly after you pass through the town of Dart.
GPS coordinates: N 39 30.640' / W 81 15.028'
Other: The campground provides no water; bring your own.
About the campground: As is the case with the Haught Run Campground, Hune Bridge does not get a lot of visitors. Weekdays see especially light use.
Why it's worth a visit: The three campsites here lie just across the Hune Covered Bridge, so it's very much unlike what you'll find in most campgrounds. It's quite charming. Situated in shady woods, it's got an old-timey feel, like the kind of place you might have stopped on the way home when piloting your horse-drawn wagon. It's easy to just pull out a lawnchair or blanket and set up on the riverbank and spend some lazy time taking in the view. When you're ready for a little more action, you can jump on the Muskingum River here; the campground is also a canoe access point. You can hike to Haught Run of the North Country National Scenic Trail. There's also a chance to learn a little history. There are two interpretive panels, one explaining the history of the covered bridge and one discussing the history of the oil and gas industry locally. In the campground area is a large oil tank with lines running out into the forest, so people can view how the oil is collected from wells in the woods.

52 Lane Farm Campground

Location: Northeast of Marietta
Season: Year-round
Sites: 4
Maximum RV length: 40 feet
Facilities: Vault toilets, picnic tables, fire rings
Fee per night: Free
Pets: Leashed pets permitted
Activities: Fishing, wildlife watching
Management: Wayne National Forest
Contact: (740) 373-9055; www.fs.usda.gov/wayne. No reservations are taken; it's first come, first served.
Finding the campground: From Marietta, follow SR 26 for about 5 miles. The campground will be on the right.
GPS coordinates: N 39 26.189' / W 81 21.517'
Other: The canoe launch offering access to the Muskingum River here was closed at last word, and was expected to remain closed because of maintenance issues.
About the campground: This is a shady campground, with a handful of picturesque sites.
Why it's worth a visit: This campground, which sits on the site of what once was the Lane family farm, is another along the Covered Bridge Scenic Byway. Like the others, it's quiet, pretty and too little used. But that works in your favor if you like solitude. You'll come across the occasional fishermen out for the day, but competition from other campers is small. It's unique in that it's adjacent

to a walnut plantation. Black walnut trees are common across Ohio, but they really thrive in the kind of conditions present here, moist bottomlands near open fields. The species' lightweight and fine-grained heartwood makes it a favorite for use in making furniture, gunstocks, and interior trim. Its large nut—contained inside a thick, husky shell—is a favorite of wildlife, so be sure to look for squirrels and white-tailed deer in this area. And pay attention to the trees themselves and you'll see evidence of one of their survival traits. The walnut is famous for its ability to produce juglone, a chemical toxic to competing plants. It secretes it through its roots to beat back species that would occupy its space. That's why you'll rarely find anything else growing under a walnut's canopy.

53 Leith Run Recreation Area

Location: North of Marietta
Season: Memorial Day weekend–mid-Oct
Sites: 21, all ADA accessible
Maximum RV length: 90 feet
Facilities: Flush toilets, water, warm showers, sanitary dump station, electricity, picnic tables, grills, fire rings, lantern hangers, boat launch, playground, volleyball courts, horseshoe pits
Fee per night: $$$ to $$$$
Pets: Leashed pets permitted
Activities: Fishing, wildlife viewing, boating, hiking
Management: Wayne National Forest
Contact: (740) 373-9055; www.fs.usda.gov/wayne. For reservations call (877) 444-6777 or visit www.recreation.gov.
Finding the campground: From Marietta, head southeast on SR 7 for 21.6 miles. The entrance to the campground will be on the right.
GPS coordinates: N 39 26.712' / W 81 09.051'
Other: This campground hosts an annual "Fishing and Fun Day" that introduces kids to fishing.
About the campground: Three of the sites are walk-in only. They're located on a peninsula of sorts jutting into the Ohio River. The rest of the campground is a loop, with a good amount of space between grassy sites.
Why it's worth a visit: Leith Run Recreation Area gets an awful lot of use, and it's no wonder. There's a lot to do. Located on the banks of the Ohio River, this is, for starters, the place to see wetland wildlife. Two observation decks, one offering a panoramic view of the Ohio River and the other overlooking the backwaters of Leith Run, give visitors the opportunity to see a great variety of birds. There's some very good fishing to be had, too. Anglers can fish the Ohio River from shore or launch a canoe or small boat at a ramp that accesses the Willow Island pool. Larger boats can get on the water at the Frontier boat ramp. Waiting to be caught are largemouth, smallmouth, spotted and white bass, channel and flathead catfish, crappies, saugers, bluegills, walleyes, and freshwater drum. Many of those same species can also be caught in a backwater estuary that's accessible from a paved walkway. Accessible piers front both the river and the estuary. Finally, be sure to spend some time hiking. The Scenic River Trail starts here. It meanders through a bottomland field, between boulders and up a hill via a series of switchbacks to rocky bluffs overlooking the river.

54 Kinderhook Horse Trail

Location: North of Newport
Season: Mid-Apr–Dec
Sites: No official sites
Maximum RV length: N/A
Facilities: Vault toilet nearby, hitching rails; corrals
Fee per night: Free
Pets: Leashed pets permitted
Activities: Horseback riding, hiking, backpacking, wildlife viewing, hunting
Management: Wayne National Forest
Contact: (740) 534-6500; www.fs.usda.gov/wayne. No reservations are taken; it's first come, first served.
Finding the campground: From Marietta, follow SR 7 northeast for 17 miles to Newport. Continue 2 miles, then turn north at the KINDERHOOK sign at CR 25. Turn right onto CR 244/Dana Road and follow that 0.8 mile to the trailhead.
GPS coordinates: N 39 24.368' / W 81 13.485'
Other: Hiking is free, but a trail permit is required of horseback riders, who are allowed to use the trails from Apr 15–Dec 15. Permits can be acquired on a daily or season basis.
About the campground: This area gets relatively light usage, so crowds are not usually a problem, especially midweek. There are some ponds nearby for watering horses, but no potable water for human consumption.
Why it's worth a visit: This is Wayne National Forest's newest trail system. It has 12 miles of trails through some of the forest's steeper, more rugged terrain. That's not to say it's wilderness; riders will pass through fields, brushland, mature forest, and regenerating forest, much of that the result of man's activities. But these are also some of the most striking landscapes in Ohio. Opportunities to see wildlife are plentiful, given all those merging habitats, so keep your eyes open for deer, coyotes, foxes, and perhaps even a black bear. A few have moved into Ohio in recent years, so maybe you'll get a glimpse of one. You might also see some other trail users. Though designed with horseback riders in mind, the trails are open to hikers and mountain bikers, too.

55 Washington County Fairgrounds

Location: South of Caldwell
Season: Year-round, though water is shut off from Nov 1–Apr 30
Sites: 100
Maximum RV length: No restriction
Facilities: Flush toilets, showers, water, electricity, sanitary dump station, picnic tables
Fee per night: $$$ to $$$$
Pets: Leashed pets permitted
Activities: Hiking, biking, fishing, boating
Management: Washington County Agricultural and Mechanical Association

Contact: (740) 373-1347; www.washcountyfair.org. No reservations are taken outside of fair week; it's first come, first served.

Finding the campground: From Caldwell, head south on I-77 toward Marietta for 19 miles. Take exit 6 toward Marietta, go 0.2 mile, then turn right onto SR 821 and go another 3.1 miles. Turn left onto SR 60 and go 1.6 miles. Turn right onto Front Street and the fairgrounds are almost immediately on the left. Follow the signs to Fair Office.

GPS coordinates: N 39 25.790' / W 81 28.049'

Other: Pets are permitted here, but the campground actually prefers if you leave them at home. You must clean up after any you bring.

About the campground: Camping is done on the honor system. You pay using envelopes you pick up and return outside the fair office.

Why it's worth a visit: This fairgrounds is right next to the Muskingum River and a boat launch, so you can stay here and hike, bike, fish, and boat. There are a number of other trails and birding areas nearby, too. But if you come here, leave yourself some time to explore the area's Underground Railroad historic sites. There are many in Washington County and in the area immediately beyond. Some are private residences and not open to the public, but many can be seen and explored. One is Blennerhassett Island State Historical Park (www.blennerhassettislandstatepark .com). It's actually in West Virginia, but it's only a short drive away. Open May–Oct, it features a museum, restored mansion, horse-drawn wagon rides, bike rentals, nature walks, and more. The fact that you get to the island via a stern-wheeler cruise makes the trip especially fun.

56 Lake Hope State Park

Location: Northeast of McArthur
Season: Year-round, though some parts of the campground are closed seasonally
Sites: 187
Maximum RV length: 50 feet
Facilities: Vault toilets, warm showers, electricity, water, sanitary dump station, laundry facilities, picnic tables, fire rings, environmental education programs, boat rental, boat launch, historical interpretive center.
Fee per night: $$$$
Pets: Permitted at some sites
Activities: Hiking, biking, backpacking, horseback riding, boating, fishing, hunting, swimming
Management: Ohio Department of Natural Resources
Contact: (740) 596-4938; www.dnr.state.oh.us/parks/parks/lakehope/tabid/754/Default.aspx. For reservations call (866) 644-6727 or visit www.ohio.reserveworld.com. Some sites are first come, first served.
Finding the campground: From McArthur, follow US 50 east for 2.7 miles. Turn left onto Powder Plant Road/SR 677 and go 3.1 miles, then turn right to stay on the same road and go another 1.6 miles. Turn right, then an almost immediate left in the town of Zaleski to stay on SR 677, then take the first left onto SR 278/Second Street; go a little more than 5 miles, then turn left onto Furnace Ridge Road and follow signs to Campground.
GPS coordinates: N 39 21.002' / W 82 20.632'

Though it stopped operating in 1874, the Hope Furnace still stands at Lake Hope State Park.

Other: This park rents sixty-six family-sized lodges, a group lodge and two camper cabins and has an organized group tenting site. A popular dining hall destroyed by fire has been rebuilt.

About the campground: This is another campground where sites are bunched up. The non-reservable sites are closest to the camp office.

Why it's worth a visit: Completely surrounded by Zaleski State Forest and taking in nearly 3,000 acres, this park has a big, rugged, and rustic feel to it. As you'd expect, natural wonders are the main attraction. The park has about 23 miles of single track mountain biking trails that, individually, range in length from a half mile to more than 7 miles. As a whole, the trail system has been rated the best in Ohio by one biking magazine. You can get a map of the trails from the park, while the Athens Bicycle Club (http://athensbicycleclub.org) offers some suggested routes. There are also more than 10 miles of hiking trails and—if you want to extend your walk—33 miles of backpacking trail, complete with shelters, in the nearby state forest. Whether you are traveling by spoked wheel, foot or even by boat in the park's quiet 120-acre lake, be sure to be on the lookout for wildlife. Beavers are common in the lake's many inlets and you can find a great blue heron rookery containing as many as fifty nests just downstream of the dam. Turkey vultures can often be seen roosting in the trees around the lake and white-tailed deer, turkeys, and woodpeckers are abundant. To get an up-close look at wildlife, visit the park nature center, which always has live animals on display.

57 Zaleski State Forest Horse Camp

Location: Northeast of McArthur
Season: Year-round
Sites: 16
Maximum RV length: N/A
Facilities: Vault toilets, picnic tables, fire rings, water, hitching posts
Fee per night: Free
Pets: Leashed pets permitted
Activities: Horseback riding, hiking, hunting
Management: Ohio Department of Natural Resources
Contact: (740) 596-5781; http://ohiodnr.com/forestry/forests/zaleski/tabid/5171/Default
.aspx. Reservations are not available; it's first come, first served.
Finding the campground: From McArthur, head east on SR 50. Just after going through the town
of Bolins Mills, turn left onto SR 356. Make a left onto Gambill Hollow Road/TR 14, then make a
right onto Bridle Path Road and follow it to the horsecamp.
GPS coordinates: N 39 16.523' / W 82 19.331'
Other: In addition to the horse camp, the Atkinson Ridge Hunter's Camp is operated seasonally,
from one day before the start of the squirrel season until one day after the close of grouse season,
and again from fourteen days before the spring gobbler season opens to one day after it closes.
Sites are first come, first served. There are latrines, picnic tables, and fire rings. It's located on
Township Road near the fire tower. To reach it, head east from McArthur on SR 50. Just after passing through Prattsville, turn left onto SR 278 north. Just before reaching the town of Zaleski, turn
right onto TH 5/Atkinson Ridge Road and follow it to the camp. GPS coordinates for the camp are
N 39 17.663' / W 82 22.143'.
About the campground: Water is not always available here. Horse owners should plan to bring
what they need, for themselves as well as their animals.
Why it's worth a visit: The Zaleski is the second largest state forest in the Ohio system at almost
27,000 acres. It's also home to the state's best-known backpack trail, also known as the Zaleski.
It's 23.5 miles if you follow the main loop, though there's also a 10-mile day loop. A map shows
the layout of the trail and outlines trail rules while also highlighting historic and natural sights you
might see along the way. That includes Zaleski flint, which was important to Native Americans as
a tool and can be found in places here. There's more to the forest than that, though. It also has
50 miles of bridle trails emanating from the horsecamp. There are grouse and turkey management
zones where the habitat is manipulated for those species, as well as the Waterloo, a 447-acre forest within the Zaleski that contains some of the tallest, oldest white pines in the state. Perhaps the
most unique thing about this forest, though, is its resident ghost. A brakeman on the B&O Railroad
was killed in the area of the Moonville tunnel around the turn of the twentieth century. Legend has
it that visitors to the tunnel today can still, on dark nights, see his lantern waving.

58 Vinton Furnace State Experimental Forest Hunting Camp

Location: East of McArthur
Season: 2 months, for a week in Nov–Dec and mid-Apr–mid-May
Sites: 3 camping areas, each capable of holding multiple campers
Maximum RV length: N/A
Facilities: Vault toilets, picnic tables, fire rings
Fee per night: Free
Pets: Leashed pets permitted
Activities: Hiking, hunting, shooting, fishing
Management: Ohio Department of Natural Resources
Contact: (740) 596-5781; http://ohiodnr.com/DNN/forests/vintonfurnace/tabid/23009/
Default.aspx. Reservations are not available; it's first come, first served.
Finding the campground: To reach the first site, travel east on SR 50 from McArthur until you can turn right/south onto Stone Quarry Road. You're at the campsite when you get to the gate across the road. To reach the second, travel south from McArthur on SR 93 until you can turn left onto SR 324 in Dundas. Turn left again on TH 6/Sam Russell Road until you can turn right onto TH 6 and reach the campsite. To reach the third, continue past the second campsite and turn left onto TH 29/Axel Ridge Road. The campsite will be on your left.
GPS coordinates: N 39 12.810' / W 82 23.837' for the first site; N 39 11.138' / W 82 24.636' for the second site; N 39 10.104' / W 82 23.781' for the third site
Other: Campers must secure a permit from the state forest to spend the night.
About the campground: The campsites have no defined sites. You simply carve out a space in the openings provided.
Why it's worth a visit: This is known as a research forest because that's what goes on here: research into forests, forest habitats, wildlife impacts, and the like. The chief issue being studied is how to restore oak trees—one of the most valuable species to wildlife and an important part of the state's multi-billion-dollar wood industry—to Ohio. Research has been going on for more than fifty years, though the state just purchased the land officially a few years ago. State officials threw their support behind the deal because the forest is billed as "one of most biologically diverse ecosystems in the United States." Vinton Furnace is home to Ohio's largest known population of bobcats, as well as timber rattlesnakes, cerulean warblers, and several rare plant species. Hunters, anglers, hikers, and others can explore it all. Be sure to check out Arch Rock, Watch Rock, the old Vinton Furnace, and Beard Cemetery while you're here.

59 Forked Run State Park

Location: South of Lottridge
Season: Apr–Dec
Sites: 146
Maximum RV length: 50 feet

A blue dasher dragonfly rests on a stem on the edge of the water at Forked Run State Park.

Facilities: Vault toilets, warm showers, sanitary dump station, electricity, water, picnic tables, fire rings, playground, boat rental, boat launch, disc golf course, basketball and volleyball courts, environmental education programs

Fee per night: $$$$

Pets: Permitted at some sites

Activities: Boating, fishing, swimming, hiking, biking, hunting

Management: Ohio Department of Natural Resources

Contact: (740)378-6206; www.dnr.state.oh.us/parks/parks/forkedrn/tabid/735/Default.aspx. For reservations call (866) 644-6727 or visit www.ohio.reserveworld.com.

Finding the campground: From Lottridge, head north on Lottridge Road for 1.1 miles. Turn right onto US 50/SR 32 east and go 4.4 miles, then merge onto SR 7 south toward Pomeroy/Gallipolis. Go 3.6 miles and turn left onto SR 681 and go 7.8 miles. Turn right into SR 124 and follow it 3 miles to the campground entrance.

GPS coordinates: N 39 05.132' / W 81 46.215'

Other: This park has three camper cabins as well as an organized group tenting area.

About the campground: The sites in this campground are fairly well spread out, with a cluster here, a cluster there. Sites 77 to 82 and 118 to 122 offer a good bit of space and privacy.

Why it's worth a visit: No settled pastoral farm country this, the area around Forked Run State Park on the West Virginia border is steep, hilly, and wild. You're as likely to see white-tailed deer, wild turkeys or perhaps even a black bear here as anywhere. This is, after all, where raiding Native Americans came to shake their pursuers and where the landscape as much as the local militia stymied Confederate raiders seeking to escape into western Virginia during the

Civil War. The forest today is not virgin timber; it was largely logged over to feed a hungry iron furnace industry more than a century ago. But it feels untouched, especially with the large Shade River State Forest bordering it. This park offers a number of ways to enjoy that. Anglers can fish Forked Run, a 120-acre lake that holds trout as well as warmwater species like bass, or the mighty Ohio River. You can launch a boat onto either, though the lake is managed with a 10-horsepower limit. There are also hiking trails.

60 Jackson Lake State Park

Location: West of Oak Hill
Season: Year-round, but with limited facilities from Nov–Mar
Sites: 34, some walk-in only
Maximum RV length: 50 feet
Facilities: Vault toilets, electricity, water, sanitary dump station, picnic tables, fire rings, horseshoe pits, boat launch, basketball and volleyball courts, games and sporting equipment available to loan for campers, playgrounds, environmental education programs, free WiFi access for campers
Fee per night: $$$$
Pets: Permitted in some sites
Activities: Boating, fishing, swimming, hunting
Management: Ohio Department of Natural Resources
Contact: (740) 682-6197 (seasonal); www.dnr.state.oh.us/parks/parks/jacksonl/tabid/748/Default.aspx. For reservations call (866) 644-6727 or visit www.ohio.reserveworld.com.
Finding the campground: From Oak Hill, head west on SR 279 for 1.3 miles. Turn right onto Tommy Been Road/CR 8 and go north for 0.8 mile. Look for the entrance to the park office and campground on the right.
GPS coordinates: N 38 54.139' / W 82 35.802'
Other: Periodically, park officials advise against swimming or wading in Jackson Lake, swallowing its water, or coming in contact with its surface because of harmful algal blooms with toxins. Check with the park for the most up-to-date advisories.
About the campground: Though small, this is a very nice campground in that there is plenty of space between sites. Some of the tent-only sites are closest to the water.
Why it's worth a visit: This is a small park, with a 242-acre lake surrounded by 106 acres of woods and fields. It's long been a nice place to relax, picnic, camp, swim, and fish. The water situation will surely impact visitation, though, if it hasn't already. But you shouldn't abandon this park altogether. The campground is still very pleasant and there are enough things to do in the immediate vicinity of the park to make this a nice place to stay. Cooper Hollow Wildlife Area is just south of the park and offers some good fishing and hunting, while the town of Jackson, just about twenty-five minutes due north of the park, has some interesting history. The Buckeye Iron Furnace State Memorial is home to a reconstructed furnace typical of the region a century ago. The site also hosts a fall festival. Visit www.buckeyefurnace.com for details.

61 Lake Alma State Park

Location: North of Wellston
Season: Year-round, but with limited facilities from Nov–Mar
Sites: 81
Maximum RV length: 50 feet
Facilities: Vault toilets, electricity, fire rings, picnic tables, water, sanitary dump station, launch ramp
Fee per night: $$$$
Pets: Permitted in some sites
Activities: Boating, fishing, hiking, biking, swimming
Management: Ohio Department of Natural Resources
Contact: (740) 384-4474 (seasonal); otherwise (740) 596-4938; www.dnr.state.oh.us/parks/parks/lakealma/tabid/752/Default.aspx. For reservations call (866) 644-6727 or visit www.ohio.reserveworld.com.
Finding the campground: From Wellston, head north on SR 93 for 0.7 mile. Turn right onto SR 349 and go about 1.5 miles, until you can turn right at the park office on a one-way road that takes you to the campground.
GPS coordinates: N 39 08.684' / W 82 30.499'
Other: This park has one camper cabin and an organized group tenting area that is, interestingly, on an island in Lake Alma accessed via a short walkway.
About the campground: The electric sites within this campground are to the east of Lake Alma, the ten non-electric sites to the west, in what constitutes almost a miniature campground of its own. Sites are fairly close together in both.
Why it's worth a visit: There was a time when coal was king in Vinton County. That's no longer true, at least not to the degree it once was. But its legacy will live on as long as Lake Alma State Park exists because coal—and coal profits—brought it into existence. Built in 1903 by the late C.K. Davis, a wealthy coal operator, Lake Alma was originally constructed as an amusement park. It boasted a large dance pavilion, outdoor theater, merry-go-round, and several other rides. It closed in 1910, at which time the City of Wellston bought the lake for a water supply. It's now leased to the state and run as a park. Visitors today won't find any carnival rides, but there's still plenty to do. The park's 60-acre lake offers very tranquil paddling. An early morning float around its edges is an exercise in stress relief, one often punctuated by encounters with wildlife like herons, muskrats, and turtles. Three hiking trails, none especially difficult, are fun, too. Starting in the main family campground and walking Sassafras Trail to Acorn Trail and back on the one-way camp road at dusk offers the chance to see white-tailed deer and turkeys.

62 Raccoon Creek Park

Location: West of Gallipolis
Season: Year-round
Sites: 6, primarily for tents only
Maximum RV length: N/A

Visitors to Raccoon Creek can usually see a fair bit of wildlife, like this robin peeking back over its shoulder.

Facilities: Vault toilets, picnic tables, fire rings, playgrounds, baseball fields, volleyball, tennis and basketball courts, badminton, horseshoe pits, canoe access, water available in the park
Fee per night: $$$$
Pets: Leashed pets permitted
Activities: Hiking, fishing, boating, sports activities
Management: Gallia County
Contact: Reservations can be made by calling (740) 379-2711; http://oomcintyreparkdistrict .org/park-history/.
Finding the campground: From Gallipolis, follow SR 141 west for 6.1 miles. Turn left onto route 775, go 2.1 miles, then turn right onto Dan Jones Road/CR 28. Go 0.5 mile to the park entrance and follow the signs to CAMPGROUND.
GPS coordinates: N 38 47.600' / W 82 20.883'
Other: This campground is not big enough to accommodate RVs, though a small pop-up trailer might fit in some sites. Either way, bring your own water or plan to get it in the park's day use areas.
About the campground: The campground is along a gravel road that winds back to Raccoon Creek. Though small, it's rarely full at any one time.
Why it's worth a visit: At more than 700 acres, Raccoon Creek is the biggest park in the Gallia County system. It's definitely a multi-use facility. It's got a mixture of woods, fields, and wetlands, so birders love it for the wide variety of species it attracts. There's some neat hiking, too. The park is home to a natural gorge—of the kind common in this corner of the state—cut by Raccoon Creek. There are a couple of scenic vistas that are worth seeing. A fitness trail will test your stamina. The

stream can also be canoed and kayaked for much of the year. Just be sure to check water levels and watch out for strainers and other hazards when on the water. Last but not least, the park is home to all kinds of playfields and playgrounds. That makes it great for picnics and, when camping, for kids. When they get bored with one activity, there's always something else for them to do.

63 Gallia County Fairgrounds

Location: East of Rodney
Season: Apr 1–Nov 1
Sites: 200
Maximum RV length: 50 feet
Facilities: Showers, flush toilets, water, electricity, sewage, free WiFi, picnic tables on request
Fee per night: $$$$
Pets: Leashed pets permitted
Activities: Events on the grounds throughout the year
Management: Gallia County Junior Fair
Contact: Reservations can be made by calling (740) 446-4120; http://galliacountyfair.org.
Finding the campground: From Rodney, go southeast on SR 588 for 0.2 mile. Take the first left onto SR 850/Rodney Pike and go 0.2 mile, then turn right onto Jackson Parkway and go 3.5 miles. The entrance to the fairgrounds and the campground will be on the left.
GPS coordinates: N 38 50.687' / W 82 14.250'
Other: Weekly and seasonal camping is also available, with special rates.
About the campground: The campground features gravel roads and grassy lots atop a hill.
Why it's worth a visit: The fairgrounds host a number of events throughout the year, so you can time a visit to coincide with any one of them. A year-round attraction located nearby is the Bob Evans Farm. Part working farm, part museum, it showcases the beginnings of the Bob Evans Restaurant chain. The 1825 farmhouse that Evans and his wife Jewel raised their children in is still here, today on the National Register of Historic Places given its history as a stagecoach stop. The farm hosts an annual festival each Oct. The county historical society runs a museum dedicated to local life, too. The French Art Colony, a multi-arts center, also draws visitors. And there's plenty of fishing and hunting to do locally.

64 Lake Vesuvius Recreation Area
Iron Ridge Campground

Location: North of Ironton
Season: Apr–Dec
Sites: 41, 3 of them ADA accessible
Maximum RV length: 45 feet
Facilities: Vault toilets, water, electricity, sanitary dump station near Oak Hill Campground on the west side of Lake Vesuvius, picnic tables, fire rings

Fee per night: $$$
Pets: Leashed pets permitted
Activities: Hiking, fishing, hunting, boating, horseback riding
Management: Wayne National Forest
Contact: (740) 534-6500; www.fs.usda.gov/wayne. For reservations call (877) 444-6777 or visit www.recreation.gov until Oct. It's first come, first served in Nov and Dec, when the Ohio gun deer season is open.
Finding the campground: From Ironton, follow SR 93 northeast for about 6 miles. Turn right onto CR 29/Ellisonville-Paddle Creek Road and follow the signs about 1 mile to the recreation area. From there, to reach the campground, go past the iron furnace and the lake, traveling uphill for another mile, then take the first left to the campground.
GPS coordinates: N 38 36.866' / W 82 37.468'
Other: One of three campgrounds in the Lake Vesuvius Recreation Area, Iron Ridge was closed for renovations in 2012, but is once again open.
About the campground: This campground is located on a mature hardwood ridge on the east side of Lake Vesuvius. Water is available for campers through early Nov.
Why it's worth a visit: Iron Ridge Campground offers the hiker a lot of options. A half-mile trail connects the campground to Lake Vesuvius and all of the day-use facilities there. But that's just the beginning. There are more than 40 miles of trails in this general area all told, with the trailheads for many located at or near the campground. If you decide to take a walk, be sure to hit Lake Shore Trail, an 8-mile loop around the lake, and the shorter trails leading to Rock House Cave, a grand, tunnel-like sandstone cave that was once used by Native Americans for shelter. There are opportunities to have fun in and on the water, too. The 143-acre Lake Vesuvius offers some pretty decent fishing for largemouth bass, crappies, bluegills, and catfish. Fishing can be done from shore or a boat, with a launch in place for those with their own crafts and canoes and paddleboats available for those who don't. There's also a swimming beach.

65 Lake Vesuvius Recreation Area Oak Hill Campground

Location: Northeast of Ironton
Season: Apr–Oct
Sites: 28, 3 of them ADA accessible
Maximum RV length: 45 feet
Facilities: Flush toilets, warm showers, sanitary dump station, water, electricity, lantern posts
Fee per night: $$$$
Pets: Leashed pets permitted
Activities: Hiking, fishing, swimming, boating, hunting, horseback riding
Management: Wayne National Forest
Contact: (740) 534-6500; www.fs.usda.gov/wayne. For reservations call (877) 444-6777 or visit www.recreation.gov until Oct. Sites are first come, first served in Nov and Dec, when the Ohio gun deer season is open.
Finding the campground: From Ironton, hear northeast on SR 93. Turn right onto CR 29/Ellisonville-Paddle Creek Road and follow the signs 1 mile to the recreation area. From there, turn

A great blue heron takes a break from looking for fish at Lake Vesuvius.

left at the entrance and go past the lake and the boat dock. The campground is approximately 1 mile farther along on the right.

GPS coordinates: N 38 36.817' / W 82 38.010'

Other: This campground was completely renovated in 2010.

About the campground: Eight of the sites are walk-in only. There is also a fifty-person group tenting area called the Two Points Group Campground.

Why it's worth a visit: Located on a ridge of mixed oaks and pines on the west side of Lake Vesuvius, this campground is the newest of the three in the Lake Vesuvius Recreation Area. It's got two new flush bathrooms, new shower houses, and a new vault toilet. The campground makes a great jumping off point for all kinds of activities. It offers access to lots of hiking, for starters. A spur that leads to Rock House Cave, a grand, tunnel-like sandstone cave that was once used by Native Americans for shelter, starts here. There are all kinds of water-based activities available at Lake Vesuvius, and in fall this is a good base camp from which to enjoy some hunting. The campground is often "staffed" by volunteer campground hosts, so if you aren't sure what to do or where best to do it, they can offer some advice.

66 Lake Vesuvius Recreation Area Pine Knob Campground

Location: Northeast of Ironton
Season: Apr–Oct
Sites: 16
Maximum RV length: N/A
Facilities: Vault toilets, water, picnic tables, fire rings
Fee per night: $$$
Pets: Leashed pets permitted
Activities: Hiking, boating, fishing, swimming, hunting, horseback riding
Management: Wayne National Forest
Contact: (740) 534-6500; www.fs.usda.gov/wayne. No reservations are taken; it's first come, first served.
Finding the campground: From Ironton, head northeast on SR 93. Turn right onto CR 29/Ellisonville-Paddle Creek Road and follow the signs for 1 mile to the recreation area. Turn left at the entrance and go past the lake and the boat dock. The campground is about 1 mile farther along this road.
GPS coordinates: N 38 37.142' / W 82 37.970'
Other: All of the sites here are walk-in only.
About the campground: This primitive campground is for tents only. It's generally thought of as an overflow area designed to ease any crowding at Oak Hill Campground.
Why it's worth a visit: This campground is short on amenities, especially compared to the adjacent Oak Hill. It's likely for that reason that it gets comparatively little use. But that's also its main attraction. From here you can access all of the same things that make the Lake Vesuvius Recreation Area so popular, but you can do it in a setting that's very tranquil. There are no crowds, there's no hum of RV engines or compressors, no light save that from campfires and lanterns. The fact that it remains open through the end of Oct makes this campground popular with people who want to explore the fall foliage from a minimalist perspective. That makes it a favorite in many ways.

67 Hanging Rock ATV/OHM Trail System

Location: Northwest of Ironton
Season: Apr 15–Dec 15
Sites: No official sites
Maximum RV length: N/A
Facilities: Vault toilets, 50 to 75 ponds of various sizes
Fee per night: Free
Pets: Leashed pets permitted

Activities: All-terrain vehicle and off-highway motorcycle riding, mountain biking, fishing, boating, hiking, hunting

Management: Wayne National Forest

Contact: (740) 534-6500; www.fs.usda.gov/wayne. No reservations are taken; it's first come, first served.

Finding the campground: From Ironton, head west on US 52 until you can turn right/north onto SR 650. Follow that for 0.75 mile until you can turn left onto Park Road 105, then follow it for 1.5 miles to the trailhead.

GPS coordinates: N 38 34.877' / W 82 43.461'

Other: The trail system is open to all-terrain vehicles and off-highway motorcycles from Apr 15 through Dec 15. A permit from Wayne National Forest is required. They can be purchased on a daily or seasonal basis.

About the campground: There are no designated sites here; you simply set up camp where you can do so safely and with the least impact. You can find some semi-permanent sites on the gravel portion of FR 105 and on its three spur roads. No camping is allowed at the paved trailhead, though, and no water is provided anywhere, so bring your own.

Why it's worth a visit: This is one of the "dispersed" camping areas on Wayne National Forest, which means there is no campground with designated sites and amenities. It is very popular, though. Two groups in particular congregate here. All-terrain vehicle riders love this area because of its many trails, some of them challenging. This area was extensively strip-mined in the 1960s and '70s. It's been reclaimed since, though steep slopes remain. Twenty-four miles of trails for all terrain vehicles and off-highway motorcycles wind around and up and down those hills, drawing lots of riders. Sportsmen also visit the Hanging Rock area with consistency. There are dozens and dozens of ponds open to fishing, ranging in size from one-half to 7 acres. Those closest to roads get fished the hardest; some in remote areas hardly ever see an angler. Fishermen can tackle them as they see fit, even using belly boats, canoes, and kayaks, if they're willing to carry them in. Anglers and, later in fall, hunters camp around those ponds, which is a fun experience.

68   Pine Creek ATV/OHM Trail System

Location: North of Ironton
Season: Mid-Apr–mid-Dec
Sites: No official sites
Maximum RV length: N/A
Facilities: Vault toilets at the Telegraph Trailhead only
Fee per night: Free
Pets: Leashed pets permitted
Activities: All-terrain vehicle and off-highway motorcycle riding, mountain biking, hiking, hunting
Management: Wayne National Forest
Contact: (740) 534-6500; www.fs.usda.gov/wayne. No reservations are taken; it's first come, first served.
Finding the campground: To reach the Wolcott Trailhead, head north from Ironton on SR 93. Just after passing through Pedro, turn left onto SR 522. Turn right onto Clinton Furnace Road/County Road 9 and go until you see the trailhead on the right. To reach the Lyra Trailhead, proceed as for

Wolcott, but continue past that parking area until you can turn right onto Taylor Dubel Road. Follow it until you can turn left onto Howard Furnace Road; look for the trailhead on the right. To reach the Telegraph Trailhead, head north on SR 93 from Ironton. Turn left onto CR 193 and go about 400 feet to the parking area.

GPS coordinates: N 38 42.497' / W 82 42.732' for Wolcott Trailhead; N 38 44.265' / W 82 43.798' for Lyra Trailhead; N 38 47.152' / W 82 37.114' for Telegraph Trailhead

Other: As at similar sites, a permit is required to ride. All those who buy one get a topographic map of the area showing the location of trails.

About the campground: There are three trailheads here that allow camping: the Telegraph, Lyra and Wolcott Trailheads. Only the Telegraph Trailhead has a vault toilet. There are no facilities at the others and no water at any of them.

Why it's worth a visit: This is another all-terrain vehicle and off-highway motorcycle trail system. It takes in 17 miles and gets heavy use. It also comes with a warning. National forest officials tells visitors to "be aware that vandalism in remote areas can be high." That's not to say that there are any more problems here than elsewhere, but rather more of a generic statement. Camp around other people and chances you'll encounter problems is probably lower. A single, unoccupied campsite is more tempting for criminals. But in either case, use some common sense. Don't leave valuables out in the open and unattended. If it's something you can't afford to lose, lock it up in a vehicle, preferably out of sight.

69 Timbre Ridge Lake

Location: Southwest of Gallipolis
Season: Year-round
Sites: No official sites
Maximum RV length: N/A
Facilities: Vault toilets, boat launch
Fee per night: Free
Pets: Leashed pets permitted
Activities: Fishing in a 100-acre lake, boating with electric motors only, hiking, wildlife viewing, hunting, swimming.
Management: Wayne National Forest
Contact: (740) 534-6500; www.fs.usda.gov/wayne. No reservations are taken; it's first come, first served.
Finding the campground: From Gallipolis, head south on SR 7 until you can turn right/southwest onto SR 218. Follow that until you can turn right into SR 790. Turn left onto CR 37/Scottown-Lecta Road, then turn right onto Forest 91 to the CAMPING AREA.
GPS coordinates: N 38 39.323' / W 82 22.934'
Other: There are a few small privately owned lots on the north side of the lake. Respect that private property and do your thing elsewhere.
About the campground: Possession of alcoholic beverages is prohibited on the dam, at the boat launch, on the lake, in the parking lots, and within 100 feet of the shore. Law enforcement officers from the park service, division of natural resources, and local sheriff's department all patrol the area periodically, so consider yourself warned.

Timbre Ridge is one of the campgrounds open year-round, which means you have the chance to see white-tailed deer in their winter coats, like this one.

Why it's worth a visit: This area features a beautiful 100-acre lake surrounded by 1,200 acres of forested hills. It sees a fair amount of people spring, summer, and fall for a variety of reasons. In spring, the cold and deep lake gets stocked with rainbow trout by the Ohio Division of Wildlife. That makes it a favorite of fishermen. In summer, some people come to swim—there's no beach, you swim at your own risk—while others come to pursue the lake's bass, bluegills, and catfish. Just be aware of special "slot" restrictions in place on the bass. Anglers can keep fish shorter than 12 inches and longer than 15, but nothing in between. Hikers also enjoy this area. There are no trails per se, but a road system—closed to vehicles—that surrounds the lake makes for some pleasant walking. You'll often see wildlife, from white-tailed deer and turkeys to waterfowl and squirrels, along the way. Hunters know that, and so this area sees a lot of use in fall from sportsmen who camp and hunt big and small game in both the national forest and the adjacent Crown City Wildlife Management Area.

70 Vesuvius Horse Trail

Location: North of Ironton
Season: Apr 15–Dec 15
Sites: No official sites
Maximum RV length: N/A
Facilities: Vault toilets at the Paddle Creek Trailhead only, corrals, hitching rails

Fee per night: Free

Pets: Leashed pets permitted

Activities: Horseback riding, hiking, hunting.

Management: Wayne National Forest

Contact: (740) 753-0101; www.fs.usda.gov/wayne. No reservations are taken; it's first come, first served.

Finding the campground: To reach the Paddle Creek Trailhead, head north from Ironton on SR 93 for about 7 miles. Turn right onto CR 29/Ellisonville–Paddle Creek Road at the Lake Vesuvius Recreation Area sign and go about 3 miles. You'll come to the Sand Hill Trailhead first. Continue on a little farther and turn left onto Township Road 245/Elkins Creek Road. It dead-ends at the Paddle Creek Trailhead.

GPS coordinates: N 38 37.873' / W 82 34.897'

Other: Camping is free, but horseback riders need a permit. They are available on a daily or season basis.

About the campground: There are three trailheads here: at Paddle Creek, Sand Hill and Johns Creek. Paddle Creek has the only restrooms and is where the camping is. It's got a large field that can accommodate twenty-five truck-and-trailer rigs. There are no parking spots per se, so use common sense on where to go.

Why it's worth a visit: The Vesuvius Horse Trail area is a beautiful one with lots to see and lots of avenues for seeing it. There are 46 miles of trail that can be covered on horseback or foot, as hiking is permitted. The trails are broken down into loops and connector trails so you can make your ride or hike as long or as short as you like. They wind through woods, past beaver dams, along old roads and past streams. But you've got to be pretty self-sufficient to experience it all. There are few creature comforts at the trailhead—not even water for the horses—so you've got to carry in whatever you need. If you can handle that, and if you're willing to carry out all that you bring in, this is a rustic adventureland.

Southwest

The southwest region of Ohio is a real mixture.

It has lots of open space in the form of state parks, nature preserves, and hunting and fishing areas. Some of them are remote, or at least feel that way when you're in them. Shawnee State Forest is home to 8,000 acres of state-designated wilderness. The gorge cut through John Bryan State Park by the Little Miami River is rugged and beautiful. Hiking and paddling there is a real favorite. Great Seal State Park and Tar Hollow State Park and State Forest aren't huge, but they have some wild-feeling hills and vistas worth exploring, too.

Farther west, this region becomes flatter and more pastoral. Lakes are seemingly everywhere. What's interesting is what's been left behind by the lakes that were here millennia ago. This is Ohio's fossil country and visitors to the parks can look for and collect rocks with imprints of plants and animals that lived in long-ago seas.

If you want to get in on the cutting edge of camping in this region, check out the Five Rivers MetroParks in Montgomery County. They've long offered opportunities for groups to camp. They just recently began allowing families to do the same. There might be some bumps to be worked out yet, but they're already worth exploring.

There's history to be seen, as well, oftentimes within the very parks where you're camping. A couple, Caesar Creek State Park and Governor Bebb MetroPark, have pioneer villages featuring authentic nineteenth-century structures. Volunteers in period clothes often "work" the sites, educating visitors about how life was lived more than a century ago. Kids love it.

Away from the parks, one must-see site is the National Underground Railroad Freedom Center. It's estimated that as many as 100,000 slaves sought freedom via the Underground Railroad in the 1800s. This center explains how the system worked, gives a glimpse of the heroes who made it possible, talks about the risks involved for slaves and others, and more. It's a fascinating story. Also in Cincinnati is a zoo, major league baseball and football, and amusement parks. The surrounding countryside has farmers markets and other attractions.

This is just a fun place to visit. Get the gang together and go find out for yourself!

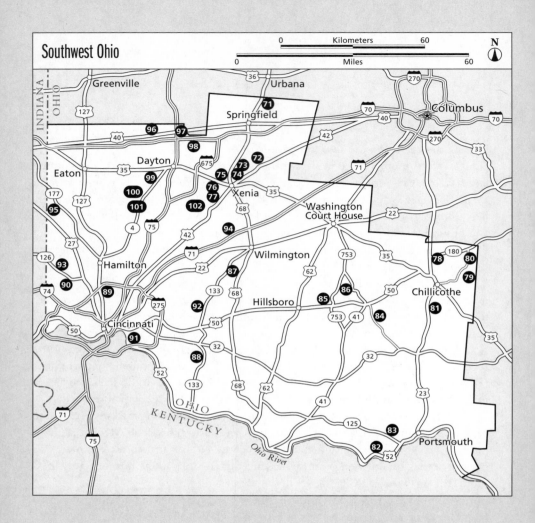

Southwest Ohio

Wide Open and Varied

	total sites	hookups	max RV lengths	toilets	showers	drinking water	dump station	recreation	fee	reservation
71 Buck Creek State Park	111	Y	35	F	Y	Y	Y	BFSLU	$$$$	Y
72 John Bryan State Park	60	Y	35	V	N	Y	Y	HBFC	$$$$	Y
73 Jacoby Road Launch	1	N	N/A	N	N	N	N	FBL	$$$-$$$$	Y
74 Old Town Reserve	1	N	N/A	N	N	N	N	HBL	$$$-$$$$	Y
75 Narrows Reserve	1	N	N/A	N	N	N	N	HFBLEE	$$$-$$$$	Y
76 Mill Bridge Launch	1	N	N/A	N	N	N	N	FBL	$$$-$$$$	Y
77 Constitution Park	1	N	N/A	N	N	N	N	FBL	$$$-$$$$	Y
78 Great Seal State Park	15	N	50	V	N	Y	N	HCRU	$$$	Y
79 Tar Hollow State Park	94	Y	50	V	Y	Y	Y	HBFSCLR	$$$$	Y
80 Tar Hollow State Forest	46	N	N/A	V	N	N	N	HRU	N/A	N
81 Scioto Trail State Park	55	Y	50	V	N	Y	Y	HBFSCL	$$$-$$$$	Y
82 Shawnee State Park	107	Y	50	F	Y	Y	Y	HBFSRL	$$$$	Y
83 Shawnee State Forest	58	N	N/A	V	N	Y	N	HFRU	N/A	N
84 Pike Lake State Park	80	Y	50	V	Y	Y	Y	HBFSEE	$$$$	Y
85 Rocky Fork State Park	171	Y	50	F	Y	Y	Y	HBFSLUEE	$$$-$$$$	Y
86 Paint Creek State Park	197	Y	50	F	Y	Y	Y	HBFSCRUEE	$$$$	Y
87 Cowan Lake State Park	254	Y	50	F	Y	Y	Y	HBFSCLU	$$$$	Y
88 East Fork State Park	389	Y	50	F	Y	Y	Y	HBFSCLRUEE	$$$$	Y
89 Winton Woods Campground	105	Y	60	F	Y	Y	Y	HBFCLEE	$$$$	Y
90 Miami Whitewater Forest	46	Y	N/A	F	Y	Y	Y	HBFCREE	$$$-$$$$	Y
91 Steamboat Bend Campground	55	Y	60	F	Y	Y	Y	HBFEE	$$$$	Y
92 Stonelick State Park	114	Y	50	F	Y	Y	Y	HBFSCLU	$$$$	Y
93 Governor Bebb MetroPark	17	N	50	V	N	Y	N	HEE	$$-$$$	N
94 Caesar Creek State Park	283	Y	40	F	Y	Y	N	HBFSCLREE	$$$$	Y
95 Hueston Woods State Park	488	Y	50	F	Y	Y	Y	HBFSCLEEU	$$$$	Y
96 Englewood MetroPark	3	N/A	N/A	V	N	N	N	HBLR	N/A	Y
97 Taylorsville MetroPark	1	N	N/A	V	N	N	N	HBFCL	N/A	Y
98 Carriage Hill MetroPark	2	N	N/A	V	N	N	N	HFREE	N/A	Y
99 Possum Creek MetroPark	2	N	N/A	V	N	Y	N	HFBR	N/A	Y
100 Germantown MetroPark	2	N	N/A	V	N	Y	N	HFB	N/A	Y
101 Twin Creek MetroPark	3	N	N/A	V	N	Y	N	HFBREE	N/A	Y
102 Sugarcreek MetroPark	2	N	N/A	V	N	Y	N	HFR	N/A	Y

See fee codes on page xx and amenities codes on page xxiii.

71 Buck Creek State Park

Location: Northeast of Springfield
Season: Year-round, but with limited facilities Nov–Apr
Sites: 111
Maximum RV length: 35 feet
Facilities: Flush toilets, warm showers, water, electricity, sanitary dump station, picnic tables, fire rings, marina, boat rentals, boat launch, disc golf course
Fee per night: $$$$
Pets: Permitted at all sites
Activities: Fishing, swimming, boating, hunting
Management: Ohio Department of Natural Resources
Contact: (937) 322-5284; www.dnr.state.oh.us/parks/parks/buckck/tabid/716/Default.aspx. For reservations call (866) 644-6727 or visit www.ohio.reserveworld.com.
Finding the campground: From Springfield, follow US 40 east for 2.2 miles. Turn left onto North Bird Road, go 1.1 miles, then continue another 0.6 mile after North Bird becomes Buck Creek Lane. Turn right onto Park Road B, which then becomes Merritt Road and follow it as it leads to the campground.
GPS coordinates: N 39 58.144' / W 83 43.487'
Other: This campground has twenty-six camping cottages. Boat camping is also permitted at designated sites.
About the campground: This is a fairly spacious campground, especially if you stay off the main spur. Sites 21 to 23 and 32 to 34 have no electricity, but are closest to the beach. You can also rent bikes from the camp office.
Why it's worth a visit: This is another park run in cooperation with the US Army Corps of Engineers, which means there's a big lake, in this case 2,120-acre C.J. Brown Reservoir. There's the requisite marina, launch ramps, beach, and fishing piers, so water lovers will find all they need. There's more to the park, though. It's home to a disc golf course that's gotten a lot of attention, as well as some nice trails, a model airplane field, a designated scuba area and, in the lake's northernmost end, some wetlands that host a variety of birds and other wildlife. Before visiting, make a point of checking out the park's local website at www.buckcreekstatepark.org. There's a wealth of information there, with some especially good tips for sportsmen. You can find details on what species of fish exist and in what numbers and sizes and get suggestions on where to fish for them and with what baits and lures. There's also information on where you can hunt and what game you might find.

72 John Bryan State Park

Location: South of Springfield
Season: Year-round, but with limited facilities Nov–Mar
Sites: 60
Maximum RV length: 35 feet
Facilities: Vault toilets, electricity, picnic tables, fire rings, water, sanitary dump station, disc golf course
Fee per night: $$$$

A young hiker climbs out of the gorge cut by the Little Miami River at John Bryan State Park.

Pets: Permitted at all sites

Activities: Hiking, road and mountain biking, boating, fishing, rock climbing and rappelling

Management: Ohio Department of Natural Resources

Contact: (937) 767-1274 seasonally; Buck Creek State Park at (937) 322-5284 otherwise; www
.dnr.state.oh.us/parks/parks/jhnbryan/tabid/750/Default.aspx. For reservations call (866) 644-
6727 or visit www.ohio.reserveworld.com.

Finding the campground: From Springfield, head south on SR 72. In the town of Clifton, turn right
onto SR 343 and follow that until you can turn left onto SR 370 south. At the first Y, turn left into
the campground.

GPS coordinates: N 39 47.365' / W 83 52.077'

Other: This park has a day lodge that can be rented spring through fall.

About the campground: This is a very nice campground. Sites are spacious, mostly shaded, and
relatively far apart in a nice setting.

Why it's worth a visit: The official literature brands John Bryan State Park as "the most scenic
state park in western Ohio." They got that right. The park is home to a remarkable limestone gorge
cut by the Little Miami River, a designated State and National Scenic River. A portion of the gorge
itself is a National Natural Landmark. There are several ways to experience it. The park is home
to a number of trails, with the North Rim and South Gorge Trails particularly nice. They follow the
Little Miami through the gorge on opposite sides and let you fish the river and hike it to look for
waterfowl, herons, and other wildlife. There are a couple of footbridges across the river, so you can
hike parts of each trail in a loop. The John L. Rich Trail, meanwhile, takes you to the stairs leading
into the gorge and the Bear's Den Interpretive Area, a nature center with hands-on displays of furs,
turtle shells, skulls, and antlers. You can also paddle the Little Miami. A launch near the park on

Jacoby Road provides access and leads past steep cliffs, historic sites, and tall sycamores. There are two dams within the park that need to be portaged, however. Finally, John Bryan offers rappelling. There are several designated rock climbing sites. You have to bring your own equipment, but there's no fee.

73 Jacoby Road Launch/Morris Bean Reserve

Location: North of Xenia
Season: Year-round
Sites: 1
Maximum RV length: N/A
Facilities: Canoe launch, picnic tables, fire rings
Fee per night: $$$ to $$$$, depending on how many are in your group
Pets: Leashed pets permitted
Activities: Canoeing, kayaking, fishing
Management: Greene County Parks District
Contact: For reservations call (937) 562-6440; www.gcparkstrails.com/parks-facilities.htm.
Finding the campground: From Xenia, head north on US 68 for 4.1 mile. Turn right onto Clifton Road and go 2.4 miles, then turn left onto Jacoby Road and go 0.4 mile to the park. Follow the signs to CAMPING AREA.
GPS coordinates: N 39 45.823' / W 83 54.171'
Other: Campers must secure a permit from the Parks District.
About the campground: This camp has no running water or restrooms.
Why it's worth a visit: Like most Greene County parks, 54-acre Jacoby Road Launch/Morris Bean Reserve offers little in the way of amenities. There might or might not even be a portable bathroom. Only one family can camp here at a time, though, so if you get the spot, it's all yours. Situated along the Little Miami River, it offers boaters a place to stay while enjoying the river. In fact, that's how many campers use this and the county's other parks. Canoeists and kayakers will spend a night here, then float down the Little Miami River to Mill Bridge, Narrows, and Constitution Parks in succession, staying a night in each. It's a nice float. The Little Miami is a lovely waterway, the first ever put in Ohio's scenic rivers program. It's also one of the Buckeye State waterways in the National Scenic and Recreational River program. If you float it there are some dams along the way you'll need to portage. It's fun, though. And fishermen can catch largemouth and smallmouth bass, catfish, rock bass, bluegills, carp, and suckers.

74 Old Town Reserve

Location: North of Xenia
Season: Year-round
Sites: 1
Maximum RV length: N/A
Facilities: Picnic tables, fire rings, picnic shelter, grill, boat launch

Fee per night: $$$ to $$$$, depending on how many are in your group
Pets: Leashed pets permitted
Activities: Hiking, canoeing, kayaking
Management: Greene County Parks District
Contact: For reservations call (937) 562-6440; www.gcparkstrails.com/parks-facilities.htm.
Finding the campground: From Xenia, head north on US 68/North Detroit Street for 2.7 miles. Turn right onto Old Springfield Pike at the park entrance and follow the signs to CAMPING AREA.
GPS coordinates: N 39 43.356' / W 83 56.122'
Other: Campers must secure a permit from the Parks District.
About the campground: This camp has no running water or restrooms. Some facilities are accessible to people with disabilities.
Why it's worth a visit: This park is a little one, encompassing just 5 acres. It offers access to the Little Miami Scenic Trail, though, and that's the big draw. The trail runs 75 miles from Springfield in the north to Newtown in the south. It is in many ways two trails in one, with this park very near the line dividing the parts. South of Spring Valley, the trail hugs the Little Miami River and is largely shaded and rural, with pass-throughs of some small towns along the way. North of Spring Valley the trail links larger cities and takes riders past some historic sites. The Xenia Station, a restored train station, is one. The Glen Helen Nature Preserve is also found along the trail's northern half.

75 Narrows Reserve

Location: South of Beaver Creek
Season: Year-round
Sites: 1, with 1 backpacking site
Maximum RV length: N/A
Facilities: Nature center, canoe launch, picnic tables, fire rings
Fee per night: $$$ to $$$$, depending on how many are in your group
Pets: Leashed pets permitted
Activities: Canoeing, kayaking, fishing, hiking
Management: Greene County Parks District
Contact: For reservations call (937) 562-6440; www.gcparkstrails.com/parks-facilities.htm.
Finding the campground: From Beaver Creek, go south on Fairfield Road/Veterans Memorial Parkway for 0.6 mile. Merge onto US 35 east via the ramp on the left toward Xenia and go 1.8 miles. Turn right onto Factory Road and go 1.2 miles. At the intersection, enter the park and follow the signs to CAMPING AREA.
GPS coordinates: N 39 41.485' / W 84 01.753'
Other: The "backpacking" site is located about 1.5 miles from the parking lot, on a path that you follow in and out.
About the campground: This camp has no running water or restrooms. Some facilities here are accessible to people with disabilities.
Why it's worth a visit: This checkmark-shaped park is Greene County's premier open space in many ways. It's the county's biggest park at 162 acres and serves as the home of its naturalist staff. It's also home to a variety of native wildlife. There's a bird-watching room at the nature center and one where furrier animals are on exhibit, too. Naturalists lead hikes and put on a number of

programs throughout the summer, and the park is site of an annual "maple sugar pancake breakfast." Nature's Trail Summer Camps are also held. And of course, hugging the Little Miami River as it does, this park offers opportunities to paddle and fish. Fishermen can catch largemouth and smallmouth bass, catfish, rock bass, bluegills, carp, and suckers.

76 Mill Bridge Launch/Bud Owens Landing

Location: West of Bellbrook
Season: Year-round
Sites: 1
Maximum RV length: N/A
Facilities: Canoe launch, picnic tables, fire rings
Fee per night: $$$ to $$$$, depending on how many are in your group
Pets: Leashed pets permitted
Activities: Canoeing, kayaking, fishing
Management: Greene County Parks District
Contact: For reservations call (937) 562-6440; www.gcparkstrails.com/parks-facilities.htm.
Finding the campground: From Bellbrook, go east on SR 725 for 0.2 mile, then take the second left onto Washington Mill Road and go 1.5 miles. Take a slight left onto Graf Mill Road and go 0.2 mile. Follow the signs to Camping Area.
GPS coordinates: N 39 38.868' / W 84 02.713'
Other: Campers must secure a permit from the parks district.
About the campground: This camp has no running water or restrooms. There are some accessible facilities.
Why it's worth a visit: This 11-acre park has no facilities. In fact, if you didn't know in advance that camping was permitted, you'd suspect it was little more than open space where you could get on the river. But camp you can. Most often, that means using a tent. Because Greene County's parks do not have "campgrounds" per se, there is no such thing as a camping pads for RVs. But the county has made allowances in the past and allowed people to set up shop here. You've got to negotiate that in advance when securing your camping permit.

77 Constitution Park

Location: Northeast of Waynesville
Season: Year-round
Sites: 1
Maximum RV length: N/A
Facilities: Canoe launch, picnic tables, fire rings.
Fee per night: $$$ to $$$$, depending on how many are in your group
Pets: Leashed pets permitted
Activities: Canoeing, kayaking, fishing
Management: Greene County Parks District

Contact: For reservations call (937) 562-6440; www.gcparkstrails.com/parks-facilities.htm.
Finding the campground: From Waynesville, head north on US 42 for 7.3 miles. Turn left onto SR 725, go 0.3 mile, then follow the signs to the park.
GPS coordinates: N 39 36.388' / W 84 00.773'
Other: Campers must secure a permit from the parks district.
About the campground: This campground has no running water or restrooms.
Why it's worth a visit: This tiny park—it's between 2 and 4 acres—is so small that it shows up on almost no maps. Nearby Walton Park does, and people looking for this one often mistake it for the other, assuming that they are in fact one place sharing two names. But that's not the case. This is the southernmost of Greene County's parks with camping, and the stopping point for people who float the river from camp to camp. Don't overlook it as a place worth a visit in its own right, though. You won't have a ton of privacy. Anyone launching a boat here will almost of necessity be in your backyard, so to speak. But for a weekend tent camping getaway, it's nice.

78 Great Seal State Park

Location: North of Chillicothe
Season: Mar–Oct
Sites: 15
Maximum RV length: 50 feet
Facilities: Vault toilets, water, picnic tables, fire rings, playground, shelter house, tether lines for horses, disc golf course
Fee per night: $$$
Pets: Permitted at all sites
Activities: Hiking, mountain biking, horseback riding, hunting
Management: Ohio Department of Natural Resources
Contact: (740) 887-4818, care of Tar Hollow State Park; www.dnr.state.oh.us/parks/parks/grt seal/tabid/738/Default.aspx. For reservations call (866) 644-6727 or visit www.ohio.reserve-world.com.
Finding the campground: From Chillicothe, head north on U.S. 23 for 3.1 miles. Turn right onto Overly Chapel Road/Hopetown Road and go 1.8 miles, then turn right into the park at the camp-ground entrance.
GPS coordinates: N 39 24.145' / W 82 56.482'
Other: Nearby Chillicothe was the first capital of Ohio, from 1803 to 1810. It was moved to Zanesville in 1811-12, back to Chillicothe, then finally to Columbus permanently in 1816.
About the campground: Horses are allowed at sites 1 through 10; the others are for non-equestrians.
Why it's worth a visit: The hills within this park, which sometimes lead to scenic vistas and are often accordingly rugged in spots, are famous in the sense that they are depicted on the Great Seal of the State of Ohio. That terrain is challenging. The park has more than 20 miles of trails—for hikers, horseback riders and mountain bikers—and you need to be fit to comfortably tackle any of them. Sugarloaf Mountain Trail, for example, climbs 2.1 miles through a forest made up largely of maples, gaining 500 feet in elevation within a quarter mile at one point. Mt. Ives Trail leads to several vistas and is just one mile, but it likewise is very challenging. But the effort can be worth

it; on clear days you can reportedly see Columbus from some of these peaks. If you want to try something different, consider the park's 18-hole disc golf course. It's a bring-your-own-equipment course, free to use, and is sometimes the site of special games and tournaments sponsored by South Central Ohio Disc Golf. For details, visit www.chillicothediscgolf.com.

79 Tar Hollow State Park

Location: North of Londonberry
Season: Year-round, but with limited facilities Jan–Mar
Sites: 94, some walk-in only
Maximum RV length: 50 feet
Facilities: Vault toilets, warm showers, water, electricity, sanitary dump station, picnic tables, fire rings, laundry facilities, camp store, games and sporting equipment available to loan for campers, bike rentals, boat launch, miniature golf course, basketball court, playground
Fee per night: $$$$
Pets: Permitted on all sites
Activities: Boating, electric motors only, fishing, backpacking, hiking, horseback riding, mountain biking, swimming
Management: Ohio Department of Natural Resources
Contact: (740) 887-4818; www.dnr.state.oh.us/parks/parks/tarhollw/tabid/792/Default.aspx. Reservations can be made by calling (866) 644-6727 or visiting www.ohio.reserveworld.com.
Finding the campground: From Londonberry, go north on SR 327 for 4.9 miles. Turn left to stay on SR 327, for 0.3 mile, then take another left to stay on SR 327 again and go 4.6 miles. Turn left onto Tar Hollow Road and go about 2 miles to the campground entrance, which will be on the left.
GPS coordinates: N 39 23.514' / W 82 45.096'
Other: This park has five backpack shelters and allows camping, by reservation, at seven picnic shelters.
About the campground: This "campground" is actually a series of nearby, but not necessarily connected, loops and even single sites, each of which goes by a different name: Pine Lake, General Cove, North Ridge, Ross Hollow and Logan Hollow Campgrounds. Sites are reservable by local sale only in Jan–Mar.
Why it's worth a visit: Tar Hollow gets its name from the shortleaf and pitch pines growing on its ridges. Early settlers took the knots and heartwood from those trees for use in everything from animal liniments to medicinal balms and wagon lubricant. Today, thanks to those hills this park is beautiful in fall when the leaves change color. Looking up at the surrounding hillside from the surface of the park's 15-acre pond is one great way to enjoy the view. Another is by hiking the park's numerous trails. The yellow-blazed Ross Hollow Hiking Trail starts near the Ross Hollow portion of the campground, so it's convenient, and winds for 3.5 miles. The 2.5-mile Pine Run Mountain Bike Trail can be biked or hiked and likewise starts near the campground's general store. It's mostly flat and is family friendly, given that there are a couple of stream crossings that are perfect for breaks to look for crayfish and bugs. And if you want do something different, visit the park on the third Sat in Sept for the annual Mountain Heritage Campout. It features hay rides, blackpowder shooting and horseshoe pitching contests, square dancing, and more.

A gray squirrel casts a wary eye after scampering up a tree at Tar Hollow State Forest.

80 Tar Hollow State Forest Horse Camp

Location: North of Londonberry
Season: Year-round
Sites: 46
Maximum RV length: N/A
Facilities: Vault toilets, picnic tables, fire rings, hitching posts
Fee per night: Free
Pets: Permitted at all sites
Activities: Horseback riding, hiking, hunting.
Management: Ohio Department of Natural Resources
Contact: (740) 663-2538; http://ohiodnr.com/forestry/forests/tarhollow/tabid/5168/Default
.aspx. Reservations are not available; it's first come, first served.
Finding the campground: From Londonberry, head north on SR 327 until you can turn left onto
Poe Run Road. Stay right at the first Y and continue until you come to the horse camp.
GPS coordinates: N 39 18.990' / W 82 46.600'
Other: State forest rules say horses can only be ridden on forest roads and designated bridle
trails.
About the campground: This camp does not have any water, so plan to bring what you need. Also
be prepared to clean up manure from your horses and dispose of it in the bins provided.

Why it's worth a visit: Tar Hollow State Forest's 16,000 acres are the result of a failed experiment. In the 1930s the government relocated farm families here, hoping they could tame the land and prosper. It didn't work. The would-be farmers couldn't make a go of it, the land was leased back to the state, and in time became the state forest. Visitors today can find lots to do here, though. Tar Hollow is home to a 26-mile network of bridle trails, all of them in the southern half of the forest. The northern half has 22 miles of hiking trails. In between and all around are 17 miles of paved roads and 14 miles of gravel ones, enough to offer up opportunities for scenic drives. This state forest is also a popular one among deer and turkey hunters. About 1,700 acres in the Coey Hollow area are being managed for grouse habitat in an effort to boost numbers of that fast, darting game bird, too. And don't forget about the mushrooms. Each Apr and May people descend on this forest to harvest some of its abundant morels. A festival each Apr celebrates the quest.

81 Scioto Trail State Park

Location: South of Chillicothe
Season: Year-round
Sites: 55
Maximum RV length: 50 feet at Caldwell Lake campground; tents only at Stewart Lake campground
Facilities: Vault toilets, water, electricity, sanitary dump station, picnic tables, fire rings, seasonal camp store, boat rentals, boat launch, basketball and horseshoe courts, games and sporting equipment available to loan for campers, environmental education programs
Fee per night: $$$ to $$$$
Pets: Permitted at all sites
Activities: Boating at two lakes, electric motors only, swimming, fishing, hiking, biking, festivals, and other special events
Management: Ohio Department of Natural Resources
Contact: (740) 887-4818, care of Tar Hollow State Park office; www.dnr.state.oh.us/parks/parks/sciototr/tabid/787/Default.aspx. For reservations call (866) 644-6727 or visit www.ohio.reserveworld.com. Some sites are first come, first served.
Finding the campground: From Chillicothe, head south on US 23 for 3.7 miles. Continue another 3.3 miles as SR 23 becomes Three Locks Road, then turn left to stay on Three Locks for another 1.5 miles. Turn right onto Stoney Creek Road and go about 3 miles until you can turn right onto Lake Road. Follow it to the campground, which will be on the left.
GPS coordinates: N 39 13.821' / W 82 57.295' for the Caldwell Lake sites; N 39 13.093' / W 82 57.781' for the Stewart Lake sites
Other: This park also rents two rustic camper cabins.
About the campground: The camping at Scioto Trail comes in two distinct units. There are eighteen non-electric, walk-in sites near Stewart Lake. There are fifty-five sites, forty of them with electricity, next to Caldwell Lake.
Why it's worth a visit: This park is surrounded by the 9,390-acre Scioto Trail State Forest, which was named for the Native American trail that ran from Chillicothe to Portsmouth. It's a great place to escape and take in some spectacular scenery. There are 12 miles of trails meant for hikers, bikers, and/or equestrians. All at least moderately difficult, they lead to a number of overlooks and

vistas of Stoney Creek and the Scioto River Valley. The woods here are very pretty in spring when full of flowering dogwood and redbud trees, and wildflowers such as Dutchman's breeches and wild blue phlox. Deborad Vista Trail is an especially nice path. You might even spot a bobcat or black bear; both are rare in the state, but have been spotted here. The park's two ponds, Stewart and Caldwell Lakes, are ideal for some quiet canoeing and kayaking. Both hold fish, including trout stocked by the state, so springtime fishing can be productive. Be sure to visit a couple of historic sites within the park, too. Near Caldwell Lake is the restored Old Log Church, a replica of the oldest Presbyterian Church in the Northwest territory.

82 Shawnee State Park

Location: West of Portsmouth
Season: Year-round, but with limited facilities from early Nov–Mar
Sites: 107
Maximum RV length: 50 feet
Facilities: Flush toilets, warm showers, water, electricity, sanitary dump station, laundry facilities, picnic tables, fire rings, boat rental, boat launch, marina, games and sporting equipment available to loan for campers, nature center, miniature golf course, playground, basketball, volleyball and horseshoe courts
Fee per night: $$$$
Pets: Permitted at all sites
Activities: Boating on two lakes, electric motors only, fishing, hiking, backpacking, horseback riding, swimming, golfing
Management: Ohio Department of Natural Resources
Contact: (740) 858-6652 park office, (740) 858-4561 campground office seasonally; www.dnr .state.oh.us/parks/parks/shawnee/tabid/788/Default.aspx. For reservations call (866) 644-6727 or visit www.ohio.reserveworld.com.
Finding the campground: From Portsmouth, head west on US 52 for 6.7 miles. Turn right onto SR 125 and go about 5.5 miles, then look for the campground entrance on the left.
GPS coordinates: N 38 43.756' / W 83 10.694'
Other: This park also has a 50-room lodge, twenty-five cottages, two camper cabins, two premium cottages, an organized group tenting area and, on adjacent state forest land, an equestrian camp. The 60-mile Shawnee Backpack Trail passes through the park, too, and there's one overnight shelter area.
About the campground: This campground has its own beach, miniature golf course, boat launch and playground.
Why it's worth a visit: Located in a part of the state sometimes called "The Little Smokies" because of its wooded hills and deep valleys, Shawnee State Park is surrounded by the largest state forest on Ohio. It has a lot to offer. For starters, its two lakes, Roosevelt and Turkey Creek, may be small, totaling just 68 acres, but they are lovely to paddle or cruise around in a rowboat. Both get stocked with trout in addition to holding bass and bluegills, so the fishing's pretty good. If you want to explore in a bigger craft, that's possible, too. The park operates a marina on the banks of the Ohio River. There's also an 18-hole golf course on site. If you want to wander the woods, there's a lot of hiking available, especially once you factor in the trails that also cross onto state forest land. The Shawnee Backpack Trail leads to some of Ohio's greatest wilderness areas, and they're worth seeing even if you do it as a day trip.

83 Shawnee State Forest Bear Lake Horse Camp

Location: South of Lombardsville
Season: Year-round
Sites: 58
Maximum RV length: N/A
Facilities: Vault toilets, picnic tables, fire rings, water, hitching posts
Fee per night: Free
Pets: Permitted at all sites
Activities: Horseback riding, hiking, backpacking, hunting, fishing
Management: Ohio Department of Natural Resources
Contact: (740) 858-6685; http://ohiodnr.com/forestry/forests/shawnee/tabid/5166/Default
.aspx. Reservations are not available; it's first come, first served.
Finding the campground: From Lombardsville, head west on SR 73 for just a short way, until you can turn left onto SR 371. At the Y, turn right onto State Forest Road 1. Make a sharp right onto State Forest Road 6 and follow it to the campground, at the junction with State Forest Road 4 and near Bear Lake.
GPS coordinates: N 38 46.886' / W 83 10.590'
Other: Shawnee State Park lies within the boundaries of the forest and offers many more amenities, so if you want to get cleaned up before heading home, its modern campground is an option.
About the campground: The campground here, known as the Bear Lake Horse Camp, is only for those with horses.
Why it's worth a visit: This is the place to come for a remote, outback experience. Shawnee State Forest, named for the Indian tribe that once inhabited the area, is the state's largest at more than 60,000 acres. At one time, parts of this area, the Vastine and Cabbage Patch Hollows, were logged and mined, with stone quarried out, carried by rail to the Ohio River, then floated to Cincinnati, where it was used in the building of many structures. That industry is long gone and things are much different today. Nearly 8,000 acres have been designated as wilderness, meaning they will see no roads or disturbances. Another 8,000 acres are managed under "back country" rules, meaning timber management can be carried out for the purpose of wildlife enhancement, but motor vehicle access is limited. There are opportunities to explore all of the forest. Shawnee is home to 60 miles of hiking trails, 60 miles of trails open to horseback riding and hiking, and 60 miles of the Buckeye backpacking trail. Several ponds—initially built as water supply dams by Civilian Conservation Corps crews in the 1930s—offer fishing. There's even a motorized tour of the forest that explores some of its habitats. Maps outlining all of those trails and routes are available from the forest office.

84 Pike Lake State Park

Location: South of Bainbridge
Season: Year-round, though facilities are limited from Oct–Apr
Sites: 80
Maximum RV length: 50 feet

Facilities: Vault toilets, electricity, water, sanitary dump station, picnic tables, fire rings, camp store, playground, showers from May through September, basketball court, horseshoe pits, games and sporting equipment available to loan for campers, boat launch, disc golf course, nature center, environmental education programs

Fee per night: $$$$

Pets: Permitted at some sites

Activities: Fishing, swimming, boating, electric motors only, hiking

Management: Ohio Department of Natural Resources

Contact: (740) 493-2212; www.dnr.state.oh.us/parks/parks/pikelake/tabid/777/Default.aspx. For reservations call (866) 644-6727 or visit www.ohio.reserveworld.com. Twenty of the sites here are first come, first served.

Finding the campground: From Bainbridge, head east on US 50 for 0.7 mile, then turn right onto Potts Hill Road and go 3.2 miles. Turn right into Pike Lake Road past the dam, crossing over Egypt Hollow Road, and look for the campground on the left.

GPS coordinates: N 39 09.493' / W 83 13.188'

Other: This park has twelve family cottages, twelve standard cottages, a group lodge and an organized group tenting area.

About the campground: This is a primitive campground, but the sites are well spaced, with those on the outside of the loops the most private.

Why it's worth a visit: Pike Lake is a small state park but, surrounded by state forest, it seems bigger than it is. What's neat is the campground and day use area. They are an unexpected glade in otherwise solid woods, a pleasant place to have some fun. The park holds a 13-acre pond that is enjoyable to paddle around and fish. There's a beach that allows swimming, too. Away from the water the park has five trails, all offering relatively easy walking over short distances; none is longer than about a mile. Pay attention while you're walking them and you may see something interesting. This park is famous for the variety of ferns, mosses, lichen, and fungi that grow here. You might also see white-tailed deer, wild turkeys, squirrels, black snakes, box turtles, raccoons, and red foxes. There's also a disc golf course, a nature center and playgrounds.

85 Rocky Fork State Park

Location: East of Hillsboro

Season: Year-round for the non-electric sites; those with electricity are open from Apr–mid-Dec. Facilities are limited Apr–early May and late Oct–mid-Dec.

Sites: 171

Maximum RV length: 50 feet

Facilities: Flush toilets, warm showers, water, electricity, sanitary dump station, picnic tables, fire rings, laundry facilities, camp store, launch ramps and docks for campers with boats, free WiFi for registered campers, miniature golf course, corn hole, basketball and volleyball courts, games and sporting equipment available to loan for campers, marina, boat rentals, nature center, environmental education programs

Fee per night: $$$ to $$$$

Pets: Permitted at all sites

Activities: Swimming, boating, unlimited horsepower, fishing, hiking, hunting

Management: Ohio Department of Natural Resources

Contact: (937) 393-4284 park office, (937) 393-3210 campground office; www.dnr.state.oh.us/parks/parks/rockyfrk/tabid/784/Default.aspx. For reservations call (866) 644-6727 or visit www.ohio.reserveworld.com.

Finding the campground: From Hillsboro, head east on SR 124 for 4 miles. Turn left onto North Shore Drive and go 1.2 miles, past the Highland County Airport. Look for the entrance to the campground on the right.

GPS coordinates: N 39 11.301' / W 83 31.763'

Other: There are also designated sites for boat camping on the lake and an organized group tenting area.

About the campground: The campground has some full-service hookups, as well as some pull-through sites. There's also a launch ramp and tie-up specifically for campers.

Why it's worth a visit: Col. Walter Hutchins was a visionary. Where other people built mills along Rocky Fork Creek and even dreamed of building a town centered on a railroad depot, he saw the area as a natural paradise. He was one of the first to push for building a lake and park here. That dream came true in 1953 when the first water poured over the dam to make Rocky Fork Lake. Today, people travel from all over to explore Rocky Fork's gorge—it's home to some fascinating caves and numerous wildflowers, including the very rare Sullivantia—and fish, swim, and boat on the 2,080-acre lake. The short Bird Observation Trail is a good hike to take with binoculars and camera. There are some special activities unique to this park worth checking out, too. Each September Rocky Fork hosts a world-class hydroplane boat racing festival, while the third weekend of Oct brings the annual Halloween campout with games, contests, and a haunted trail.

86 Paint Creek State Park

Location: South of Greenfield

Season: Year-round, but with limited facilities and no reservations taken mid-Oct–Apr

Sites: 197

Maximum RV length: 50 feet

Facilities: Flush toilets, hot showers, sanitary dump station, electricity, water, picnic tables, fire rings, laundry facilities, games and sporting equipment available to loan for campers, basketball and volleyball courts, horseshoe pits, boat rentals; boat launch, nature center, bird observatory, environmental education programs, disc and miniature golf courses

Fee per night: $$$$

Pets: Permitted at some sites

Activities: Boating, fishing, swimming, hiking, horseback riding, mountain biking, hunting, rock climbing

Management: Ohio Department of Natural Resources

Contact: (937) 981-7071 camp office seasonally; (937) 393-4284 Rocky Fork Park office otherwise; www.dnr.state.oh.us/parks/parks/paintcrk/tabid/776/Default.aspx. For reservations call (866) 644-6727 or visit www.ohio.reserveworld.com.

Finding the campground: From Greenfield, go east on SR 28 for 1 mile. Turn right onto SR 41 south, go 5.1 miles, then turn right onto Cliff Run Road/TH 6H and go .09 mile. Take the first right onto Chambliss Road/TH 3T, go 1.6 miles, and turn left onto Rapid Forge Road. Travel less than 1 mile, then turn right onto Taylor Road/TH 2. Take the first left at the signs to CAMPGROUND.

GPS coordinates: N 39 16.170' / W 83 23.107'

Other: A primitive horseman's camp is available for those who bring their own mounts. The park also rents two deluxe camper cabins.

About the campground: This is a family-friendly campground, with basketball courts, a volleyball court, horseshoe pits and a playground, all within walking distance of each site.

Why it's worth a visit: Paint Creek is a dividing line. Situated on the very edge of the Appalachian plateau, it separates the hilly eastern section of Ohio from the flatter country to the west. Straddling those two worlds, it offers a diversity of plants and wildlife. It's known as much as anything for its wildflowers. It was thought to be home to as many species as anywhere before the dam flooded much of the valley. Still today, you can see wild geranium, jewelweed, yarrow, and Queen Anne's lace in the park's woods and meadows. Outside but very near the park, in a gorge cut by Rocky Fork Creek in the state park by the same name, you can even find the very rare Sullivantia, marked by shiny leaves and small white flowers, blooming in mid-summer. Check out the "Seven Caves" along the creek, too. While in Paint Creek, also visit the nature center, with its displays of local fish and wildlife, and spend some time on the nearly 1,200-acre lake. You can swim, fish and boat, with no horsepower restrictions.

87 Cowan Lake State Park

Location: South of Wilmington

Season: Year-round

Sites: 254, some ADA accessible

Maximum RV length: 50 feet

Facilities: Flush toilets, warm showers, electricity, sanitary dump station, water, picnic tables, fire rings, laundry facilities, marina with boat rental, boat launch, camp store, bike rental, miniature golf course, playground

Fee per night: $$$$

Pets: Permitted at all sites

Activities: Fishing, hiking, mountain biking, hunting, swimming, golf, boating, with a 10-horsepower limit

Management: Ohio Department of Natural Resources

Contact: (937) 382-1096 park office; (937) 383-3751; www.dnr.state.oh.us/parks/parks/cowanlk/tabid/722/Default.aspx. For reservations call (866) 644-6727 or visit www.ohio.reserve world.com.

Finding the campground: From Wilmington, head south on US 68 for 3.7 miles. Turn right onto West Dalton Road, go 0.1 mile, then take the first left to stay on West Dalton. Go 1.6 miles. Turn right onto Osborn Road, then turn left at the signs for CAMPGROUND.

GPS coordinates: N 39 23.283' / W 83 52.988'

Other: This park also rents twenty-seven cottages and two premium cottages and has two organized group tenting areas.

About the campground: Rare are the sites that aren't very near another. You can, though, pick sites close to hiking or mountain bike trails. Reservations are taken only locally Nov–Mar.

Why it's worth a visit: Cowan Lake is not the biggest in the state park system, but it can be one of the prettiest. At certain times of the year, when American lotus water lilies are in bloom, floating on the surface with their dark green leaves and bright yellow flowers, the lake is a beautiful place to paddle. These kinds of flowers are otherwise rare in such densities in this part of the world. But here you'll know them when you see them: Their leaves can reach 2 feet in diameter. When you're on the lake, try your hand at fishing and watch for sailboats, too. A lake map—see it at www.dnr.state.oh.us/Home/ FishingSubhomePage/LakeMapLandingPage/CowanLakeFishingMap/tabid/19504/Default.aspx— offers tips on lake depths, bottom contours and more to help you find fish. The sailboats, meanwhile, will likely belong to a club based here that stages events and competitions. They're fun to watch.

88 East Fork State Park

Location: East of Batavia
Season: May–Dec
Sites: 389
Maximum RV length: 50 feet
Facilities: Flush toilets, warm showers, electricity, water, sanitary dump station, picnic tables, fire rings, environmental education programs, boat launch, miniature golf course, playgrounds
Fee per night: $$$$
Pets: Permitted at all sites
Activities: Boating, unlimited horsepower, hiking, horseback riding, golfing, mountain biking, backpacking, fishing, swimming, hunting
Management: Ohio Department of Natural Resources
Contact: (513) 734-4323 park office; (513) 724-6521 campground, seasonal; www.dnr.state.oh .us/parks/parks/eastfork/tabid/732/Default.aspx. For reservations call (866) 644-6727 or visit www.ohio.reserveworld.com.
Finding the campground: From Batavia, head east on Old SR 32 for 4.3 miles. Take the first right past Afton–Elk Lick Road and follow the signs to CAMPGROUND.
GPS coordinates: N 39 03.145' / W 84 06.283'
Other: Ohio's Departments of Natural Resources and Agriculture are trying to stop the spread of the Asian Longhorned Beetle and have identified East Fork and Stonelick State Parks as infested areas. That means firewood can be brought into the parks, but cannot be taken out. There's an equestrian camp with seventeen electric sites, as well as four camper cabins and four cedar cabins and several backcountry campsites.
About the campground: This campground is a series of loops, each with individual sites crammed pretty close together. Camping loop C does have a little more space, however.
Why it's worth a visit: One of Ohio's largest state parks and just 25 miles from Cincinnati, East Fork gets a lot of use. People come to swim, picnic, and more. Two attractions stand out above all others, though. One is the park's lake. Unlimited horsepower boating is allowed, so there's a lot of skiing, tubing, and racing on personal watercraft that goes on. People also fish the lake. Some of the narrower fingers off the main channel hold good populations of bass and crappies. The park's other main attraction is its trails; they are numerous and varied. You can hike loop trails as short as a half mile or circle the entire lake on the 32-mile Steven Newman Worldwalker Perimeter Trail. Open to hikers, equestrians, and backpackers, it's home to four primitive campsites all its own.

A pink water lily floats on the water at Winton Woods.

They're free to use so long as you get a permit from the park office. There's also a second, 14-mile backpack trail worth exploring, even if you do just a portion as a day hike.

89 Winton Woods Campground

Location: North of Cincinnati
Season: Mar–Nov
Sites: 105
Maximum RV length: 60 feet
Facilities: Flush toilets, warm showers, electricity, water, sewage, sanitary dump station, picnic tables, fire rings, camp store, laundry facilities, WiFi, boat rental, boat launch, playground, disc golf course, environmental education and other programming
Fee per night: $$$$
Pets: Leashed pets permitted
Activities: Fishing, boating, disc golfing, hiking, biking
Management: Hamilton County Park District
Contact: For reservations call (513) 851-2267; www.hamiltoncountyparks.org/recreation/camping/winton-woods-campground.html.
Finding the campground: From Cincinnati, head north on I-75 for 5.6 miles. Take the Mitchell Avenue exit, exit 6, and go 0.1 mile, keep left to take the Mitchell Avenue ramp, then turn left onto West Mitchell Avenue and go 0.4 mile. Turn left onto Spring Grove Avenue and go 0.4 mile. Turn

right onto Winton Road and go 6.7 miles, then turn left onto Lakeridge Road. The entrance to the campground will be on the left at McKelvey Road.

GPS coordinates: N 39 15.147' / W 84 30.155'

Other: The maximum length of stay at any one site is fourteen days.

About the campground: This park also rents camping cabins and deluxe cabins, which offer everything from TV to air conditioning.

Why it's worth a visit: Just twenty minutes north of downtown Cincinnati, this campground sits within a 2,554-acre park, making it an oasis of green outside one of Ohio's urban centers. A lot of the usual outdoor activities go on here. There's fishing in 188-acre Winton Lake, boating—with tour boat rides offered on weekends, weather permitting—hiking, disc golf, and more. Some of the hiking can be done on a fitness trail, which includes exercise equipment at assorted stations. Something unique about this park is the presence of the Winton Woods Riding Center. Beginners can learn to ride horses, in the western, contesting, jumping, dressage, or hunt seat styles, in private or semi-private lessons. If you are already familiar with riding, there are opportunities to do rides on a 2.6-mile trail. There are usually about thirty-five horses here at any one time. A number of horse- and riding-related shows and events are held throughout the summer, so there's always something equine going on.

90 Miami Whitewater Forest

Location: Northwest of Cincinnati

Season: May–Dec

Sites: 46

Maximum RV length: No restriction

Facilities: Flush toilets, warm showers, electricity, water, sanitary dump station, picnic tables, fire rings, playground, boat rental, 18-hole golf course, disc golf course, nature center and gift shop, soccer and softball fields, environmental education and other programs

Fee per night: $$$ to $$$$

Pets: Leashed pets permitted

Activities: Fishing, boating, hiking, biking, horseback riding, golfing

Management: Hamilton County Park District

Contact: For reservations call (513) 367-9632; www.hamiltoncountyparks.org/recreation/camping/miami-whitewater-forest-campground.html.

Finding the campground: From Cincinnati, head north on I-75 toward Dayton for 3.4 miles. Merge onto I-74W/US 52W toward Indianapolis via exit 4 and go 11.5 miles. Take the SR 128 exit, exit 7, toward Cleves/Hamilton for 0.3 mile. Turn right on SR 128/Hamilton Cleves Road and go 3.1 miles, then turn left onto Mt. Hope Road and go 0.3 mile. Take the first right to stay on Mt. Hope. Pass the golf course and Habor Ridge Drive on the left. Follow it and the signs to the campground.

GPS coordinates: N 39 15.395' / W 84 45.015'

Other: This park also has a youth camp available for rent to groups.

About the campground: The sites here are all wooded and spacious, with gravel pads for parking. Sites 112 to 115 offer the most privacy.

Why it's worth a visit: This is the place in Hamilton County to visit if you want solitude amidst big woods. Miami Whitewater Forest Park takes in 4,343 acres and is the biggest park in Hamilton County. Fittingly, if there's an outdoor activity you can think of, chances are you can do it here.

Take the hiking, for example. You can walk the fitness trail and exercise on the training equipment or walk the 7.8-mile Shaker Trace Trail, which winds through and past wetlands, prairie, farmland, and creek beds. Interestingly, during summer, park ranger "courtesy carts" patrol that latter trail, handing out cold water to hikers. You can also boat on the park's 85-acre lake, ride horses on two equestrian trails, play golf on the 18-hole course or take the kids to the Parky's Pirate Cove "wet" playground on the lake, which is a favorite with the younger set. The park's visitor center is also worth checking out. It's home to a life-size, animated John James Audubon, a wetlands display with live animals and interactive displays on flight.

91 Steamboat Bend Campground/Woodland Mound and Park

Location: Southeast of Cincinnati
Season: Apr–Oct
Sites: 55
Maximum RV length: 60 feet
Facilities: Flush toilets, warm showers, electricity, water, sanitary dump station, picnic tables, fire rings, nature center, fitness trails, playground, gift shop, environmental education programming and other events, golf course, disc golf
Fee per night: $$$$; sites are only available weekly, monthly, and seasonally
Pets: Leashed pets permitted
Activities: Fishing, though not from shore, boating, hiking, golfing
Management: Hamilton County Park District
Contact: For reservations call (513) 851-2267; www.hamiltoncountyparks.org/recreation/camping/steamboat-bend.html.
Finding the campground: From Cincinnati, take I-471 south for 5.4 miles. Merge onto I-275 east via the exit on the left and go 3.9 miles. Take exit 71 toward US 52 east via the ramp on the left toward New Richmond. Go 3.4 miles, then turn left onto Eight Mile Road. Make the first right onto Old Kellogg Road and the campground.
GPS coordinates: N 39 01.849' / W 84 19.742'
Other: The maximum length of stay at any one site is 14 days.
About the campground: This campground does not allow tenting; it's open only to self-contained recreational vehicles. Most of the tree-lined sites offer a panoramic view of the Ohio River.
Why it's worth a visit: This campground is a little bit different. It doesn't cater to the weekend crowd. Rather, campers here are ones who come to stay for a week, if not much longer. Many campers here have to worry about cutting the grass around their site, they move in for so long. But there's a lot of room to roam and plenty to keep you busy. At 1,030 acres, Woodland Mound and Park, which surrounds the campground, is fairly large. Its Seasongood Nature Center is a real treat. It's home to a life-size replica sycamore tree that has doors; open them and you find birds and animals and information on each. There's an outdoor observation deck, too, along with a wild bird viewing area. Special programs held at the center throughout the camping season focus on the curiosities of nature. If that's not enough, the park is home to an 18-hole golf course, as well as a disc golf course for those who prefer flying discs to irons and woods.

The calm waters of Stonelick Lake offer opportunities for quiet paddling in Stonelick Lake State Park.

92 Stonelick State Park

Location: South of Blanchester
Season: Year-round
Sites: 114
Maximum RV length: 50 feet
Facilities: Flush toilets, warm showers, electricity, water, sanitary dump station, picnic tables, fire rings, camp store, laundry facilities, volleyball and basketball courts, horseshoe pits, tetherball, playground, games and sporting equipment available to loan for campers, bike rental, boat rental, boat launch
Fee per night: $$$$
Pets: Permitted on some sites
Activities: Biking, boating, electric motors only, fishing, swimming, hiking, hunting
Management: Ohio Department of Natural Resources
Contact: (513) 734-4323, care of East Fork Park office; www.dnr.state.oh.us/parks/parks/ stonelck/tabid/789/Default.aspx. For reservations call (866) 644-6727 or visit www.ohio .reserveworld.com.
Finding the campground: From Blanchester, follow SR 133 southwest for 5.8 miles. Stay straight to go on SR 727 for 2.4 miles, then turn left onto Newtonsville Road. Go 0.1 mile, then take the first left onto Lake Drive. Go past the park office and continue until you see the campground entrance on the left.

GPS coordinates: N 39 13.025' / W 84 03.532'

Other: Ohio's Departments of Natural Resources and Agriculture are trying to stop the spread of the Asian Longhorned Beetle and have identified Stonelick State Park as an infested area. As a result, firewood can be brought into the park but not taken out. The park also rents a deluxe camper cabin and has an organized group tenting area.

About the campground: This campground sits on the shores of Stonelick Lake and is for the most part very nice, with the sites on the north end of the campground the most spacious.

Why it's worth a visit: This picturesque park is another of those in Ohio that is well known for the fossils it gives up. People have been coming here since the 1800s to search for and find the stone imprints of ancient plants and sea animals. A talk to the folks in the park office can give you tips on where to start your search. Be sure to pay some attention to the forest here, too. In most places, sweet gum trees are a subordinate species, filling gaps in the woods not already taken, but never predominating on their own. That's not the case here. The park is home to a significant stand of sweet gums that—together with beech and maples—hold sway among other trees. There are some nice wildflowers to see, too, such as flying star, Virginia mountain mint, and purple fringeless orchid. Four multi-use trails that wind through the park are avenues for seeing all of those things. Don't overlook opportunities to fish and boat on 200-acre Stonelick Lake either. Smooth as glass some days, with only oar strokes disturbing the surface, it's a lot of fun to explore.

93 Governor Bebb MetroPark

Location: West of Millville
Season: Year-round
Sites: 17
Maximum RV length: 50 feet
Facilities: Vault toilets, picnic tables, fire rings, water (within the park, but not in the campground), playground, environmental education programming
Fee per night: $$ to $$$
Pets: Leashed pets permitted
Activities: Hiking, pioneer village
Management: MetroParks of Butler County
Contact: (513) 867-5835; www.yourmetroparks.net/index.cfm?page=park_GovBebb. No reservations accepted; it's first come, first served.
Finding the campground: From Millville, go west on SR 129 for 8.7 miles. Take a sharp left onto Cincinnati Brookville Road/SR 126 and go 1 mile. Turn right onto Bebb Park Lane to enter the park and follow the signs to CAMPGROUND.
GPS coordinates: N 39 22.364' / W 84 48.261'
Other: This park also has a youth hostel and two organized group camping areas for which reservations can be made.
About the campground: All firewood used in the campground must be purchased here. There's no electricity yet, but there are plans to install it in time.
Why it's worth a visit: A visit to Governor Bebb MetroPark is a step back in time. At the entrance to the park is an 1850 covered bridge—one of two remaining in the county—that was rebuilt in 1970. But that's the baby of the other structures here. The park takes its name from William Bebb, the

The pioneer village at Caesar Creek State Park features fifteen buildings that date to the 1800s.

nineteenth governor of Ohio. His 1799 birthplace cabin and boyhood home serves as the center-piece of this park's Pioneer Village. It's a collection of seven authentic log cabins and other buildings from around the region that have been collected and reassembled here to show visitors what a representative early Midwestern settlement looked like. There's a blacksmith shop, schoolhouse, and tavern among the buildings. The village is often "staffed" by volunteers in period clothes throughout the summer, when a number of different educational programs are offered for the public. A brochure available from the park describes each building and outlines a walking tour of the village. There are also a number of hiking trails, some winding through woods, others through meadows.

94 Caesar Creek State Park

Location: East of Waynesville
Season: Year-round, but with limited facilities Jan–Mar
Sites: 283
Maximum RV length: 40 feet
Facilities: Flush toilets, warm showers, electricity, water, picnic tables, fire rings, playground, nature center, environmental education programs, boat launch
Fee per night: $$$$
Pets: Permitted at all sites
Activities: Boating, hiking, mountain biking, horseback riding, fishing, swimming

Management: Ohio Department of Natural Resources
Contact: (937) 382-1096 Cowan Lake State Park; (937) 488-4595 campground office; www.dnr
.state.oh.us/parks/parks/caesarck/tabid/720/Default.aspx. For reservations call (866) 644-
6727 or visit www.ohio.reserveworld.com.
Finding the campground: From Waynesville, head east on SR 73 a little more than 5 miles, then
turn left onto Brimstone Road. Turn left onto Ward Road/TH 128 to reach the campground.
GPS coordinates: N 39 32.259' / W 83 58.607'
Other: This park has a camp with thirty sites for equestrians. All are available on a first come, first
served basis. The park also has two camper cabins and two cedar cabins and several group campsites.
About the campground: This campground has a number of amenities, from playgrounds and basketball courts to an amphitheater, beach and changing house. Reservations are by local sale only
in Jan–Mar.
Why it's worth a visit: Caesar Creek is one of the top spots for outdoor recreation in southwestern
Ohio, and with good reason. It has 3,741 acres of woods and fields around a 2,830-acre lake.
That waterway offers some of the best crappie fishing in the state, as well as opportunities to
catch smallmouth, largemouth and spotted bass, saugeyes, muskies, and more. You can get at
them from a boat or 42 miles of shoreline featuring coves, stumps, and standing trees. There's
also a special pond open only to kids sixteen and younger. Away from the water there are miles of
trail. The Spillway Trail that begins at the Wellman Meadows boat ramp leads to a spillway overlook
and a waterfall. Caesar Creek Gorge Nature Preserve, meanwhile, though not technically a part of
the park, is adjacent to it and offers some wonderful hiking through a deep gorge. Worth exploring,
too, is Caesar Creek's pioneer village. It's a living history museum featuring seventeen buildings
that date to the late 1700s and early 1800s. Visitors can walk through it during daylight hours
or visit during special events like the gospel festival, Native American gathering and Civil War re-
enactment. Visit www.caesarscreekpioneervillage.org/ for details.

95 Hueston Woods State Park

Location: North of Oxford
Season: Year-round, but with no showerhouse and limited facilities from Dec–Mar
Sites: 488
Maximum RV length: 50 feet
Facilities: Flush toilets at the sites with electricity, rustic toilets at the others, warm showers, sani-
tary dump station, water, picnic tables, fire rings, laundry facilities, horse riding arena, free WiFi
for campers, disc golf course, paintball field and range, boat launch, archery range, miniature golf,
nature center, environmental education programs
Fee per night: $$$$
Pets: Permitted at all sites
Activities: Hiking, mountain biking, swimming, horseback riding, boating, fishing, golfing, hunting,
shooting
Management: Ohio Department of Natural Resources
Contact: (513) 523-6347 park office; (513) 523-1060 seasonal campground office; www.dnr
.state.oh.us/parks/parks/huestonw/tabid/745/Default.aspx. For reservations call (866) 644-
6727 or visit www.ohio.reserveworld.com.

Sailing is a popular activity at Hueston Woods State Park.

Finding the campground: From Oxford, head north on Brown Road for about 4.5 miles. Turn left onto Main Loop Road and follow the signs for Campground.

GPS coordinates: N 39 35.145' / W 84 46.076'

Other: There is a ninety-four-room lodge and conference center, twenty-five family cottages, two premium cottages, ten efficiency cottages and three camper cabins, as well as an equestrian campground that has twenty electric and five non-electric sites. They're available on a first come, first served basis.

About the campground: This campground is a crowded one, with lots of sites packed tightly against another. The miniature golf course is located in a picnic area between camp areas 3 and 4.

Why it's worth a visit: A visit to Hueston Woods offers two ways to get a glimpse of Ohio's past. First, there's the park's limestone bedrock. This area was once under a shallow sea and that magnesium-bearing dolomite rock offers proof in the form of marine animal fossils. People from all over the world come to the park's two designated fossil collection areas, one at each end of the lake, to explore. The state's Division of Geological Survey publishes a field guide, "Fossils of Ohio," that you might want to pick up before arriving. It will help you identify what you're seeing. The park staff regularly leads field trip-style programs to this area, too. But whether you explore on your own or with a group, bring a bag; it's possible to keep what you find. The park's second peek at history comes from a stand of virgin timber. Most of Ohio's forests were cut over by early settlers, but this 200-acre stand of beech and sugar maple somehow survived. The trees tower over ferns and wild-flowers, effectively shading out any other competition. The stand has been designated a National Natural Landmark. The park staff can tell you how best to see it.

96 Englewood MetroPark

Location: West of Huber Heights

Season: Year-round

Sites: 3, for tents only, each holding 25 to 35 people

Maximum RV length: N/A

Facilities: Vault toilet, picnic tables, fire rings, boat ramps, disc golf course, nature center, garden

Fee per night: Free

Pets: Leashed pets permitted

Activities: Hiking, canoeing and kayaking, electric motorboating, horseback riding, disc golf

Management: Five Rivers MetroParks

Contact: For reservations call (937) 277-4374; www.metroparks.org/Parks/Englewood/Home.aspx.

Finding the campground: From Huber Heights, head west on I-70 for 7.5 miles. Take exit 29 onto SR 48 north and go about 1 mile until you can turn right onto West National Road. Follow that past the first parking lot until you can turn left onto Frederick Pike. Take the first left onto Patty Road and follow the signs for Old National Campground.

GPS coordinates: N 39 53.035' / W 84 16.658'

Other: Due to the threat of the emerald ash borer you can't bring firewood to any MetroPark facility. A limited supply of firewood is provided.

About the campground: All of the campsites in each of Five Rivers' parks were open only to groups until just a few years ago. Families are now permitted, but the "camps" are still relatively primitive in that they're open, mowed fields.

Why it's worth a visit: Englewood MetroPark gets a lot of visitors, but then it's got a lot to offer. It's divided into four sections: North, South, East, and West Parks. East Park is the biggest of the four and holds a couple of unique natural features. There are two waterfalls, Patty Falls and Martindale Falls, both accessible by walking less than a mile over mostly level terrain. There's also a remnant swamp forest, remarkable because of its black ash, swamp white oak, and pumpkin ash trees. Pumpkin ash in particular are otherwise very rare in Ohio. An elevated boardwalk extends into the forest so that visitors can see this stand. This is also the part of the park that has the greatest number and variety of hiking trails. North Park, meanwhile, offers access to the Stillwater River and has five ponds, four of which are open to fishing. One allows electric motorboats. West Park has hiking and more fishing and river paddling, while South Park is home to the Aullwood Audubon Center and Aullwood Garden. The latter is a serene 31-acre collection of color and scent worth visiting.

97 Taylorsville MetroPark

Location: West of Huber Heights
Season: Year-round
Sites: 1, for tents only, capable of holding 35 people
Maximum RV length: N/A
Facilities: Vault toilet, picnic tables, fire rings, boat launch
Fee per night: Free
Pets: Leashed pets permitted
Activities: Hiking, biking, fishing, canoeing, and kayaking
Management: Five Rivers MetroParks
Contact: For reservations call (937) 277-4374; www.metroparks.org/Parks/Taylorsville/Home.aspx.
Finding the campground: From Huber Heights, head west on Taylorsville Road for 1.7 miles. Turn right onto Bridgewater Road, go 0.7 mile, then take a slight left onto US 40. Go about 0.4 mile and the entrance to the two campgrounds will be on the left.
GPS coordinates: N 39 52.322' / W 84 09.625'
Other: Due to the threat of the emerald ash borer, you can't bring firewood to any MetroPark facility. A limited supply of firewood is provided.
About the campground: This park has two campgrounds, Canal View and Shumard. They share a common parking area off Bridgewater Road.
Why it's worth a visit: The Great Miami River bisects this park from north to south and is popular with paddlers. A fun trip is to set up camp here, drive upriver, then float back to the park to spend the night. You can make much the same trip parallel to the water using the bikeway. It's 7 miles of paved pathway open to hikers, skaters, and bicyclists. There are points of interest along its length. Start at the north end of the bikeway and you can explore what used to be Tadmor, once the county's busiest community before being hit by hard times and then being wiped out by flood. Around the Taylorsville Dam at the bikeway's midpoint stand remnants of Miami-Erie Canal. The hand-dug "big ditch" took twenty years to complete and was an impressive and economically important work for its day, connecting the Ohio River at Cincinnati with Lake Erie at Toledo. It's long gone, but a few pieces of it can still be seen. South of the dam the bikeway leads to a raised observation deck that overlooks a prairie. On the east side of the park, meanwhile, are two overlooks and an

interesting rock outcrop. The latter is a short walk north of the Civilian Conservation Corps shelter. In 1984 an estimated 375 tons of rock came tumbling down when the soft underlying rock gave way. In 1996 another 100 tons fell. Much smaller slides have occurred in the years since. Visitors can see some of that jumbled rock and walk up a set of stone steps and take a look at how water continues working on the cliff even now.

98 Carriage Hill MetroPark

Location: East of Vandalia
Season: Year-round
Sites: 2, for tents only, each capable of holding 35 people
Maximum RV length: N/A
Facilities: Vault toilet, picnic tables, fire rings, gift shop, stables, historical farm, environmental education programming
Fee per night: Free
Pets: Leashed pets permitted
Activities: Horseback riding, fishing, hiking
Management: Five Rivers MetroParks
Contact: For reservations call (937) 277-4374; www.metroparks.org/Parks/CarriageHill/Home .aspx.
Finding the campground: From Vandalia, follow I-75 south for 1.5 miles. Merge onto I-70 east via exit 61 toward Columbus and go 5.3 miles. Take exit 38 toward Huber Heights and follow Brandt Pike/SR 201 north for 0.9 mile. Turn right on Shull Road to enter the park. Take the first left onto Bellfontaine Road and follow it to the campground.
GPS coordinates: N 39 52.825' / W 84 04.306'
Other: Due to the threat of the emerald ash borer, you can't bring firewood to any MetroPark facility. A limited supply of firewood is provided.
About the campground: All Five Rivers MetroParks offer free camping year-round. Park officials have been talking about charging fees at some point, though, so be sure to ask when making reservations. Also be aware that there's been talk of closing some sites in winter, or at least not plowing the roads leading to them.
Why it's worth a visit: Two things really stand out about Carriage Hill MetroPark. One is its historic farm. The Daniel Arnold Family originally settled this area in 1830. The farm that remains is meant to replicate the life they would have known. There's an original log house, blacksmith and engine shops, an icehouse, poultry house, log barn, sawmill, and more. Farm animals like those the Arnolds would have raised and volunteers dressed in period clothes doing farm chores like baking bread complete the scene. A visitor center has exhibits, an interactive children's center and gift shop, while the Carriage Hill Gallery has rotating agricultural photographic and art displays. Carriage Hill's other unique feature is its horseback riding center. This stable caters to people of all experience levels. There are hand-led pony rides for especially small children on weekends and trail rides for those who are older. You can sign up to take lessons or attend youth, adult and family horse camps. If you want to try something different, this park is also home to more than 7 miles of trails for hiking, two catch-and-release ponds for fishing, and several areas of woods and fields for birding.

99 Possum Creek MetroPark

Location: Southwest of Dayton
Season: Year-round
Sites: 2, for tents only, each capable of holding 100 or more people
Maximum RV length: N/A
Facilities: Vault toilet, water, picnic tables, fire rings, farm
Fee per night: Free
Pets: Leashed pets permitted
Activities: Fishing, boating, horseback riding, hiking, birding, maple sugaring
Management: Five Rivers MetroParks
Contact: For reservations call (937) 277-4374; www.metroparks.org/Parks/PossumCreek/Home
.aspx.
Finding the campground: From Dayton, follow US 35 west toward I-75 for 3.2 miles. Take the
Gettysburg Avenue exit, go 0.3 mile, then turn left onto South Gettysburg Avenue and go 1.8 miles.
Turn right onto Frytown Road and go 0.6 mile. The entrance to the Sᴄᴀᴍᴏʀᴇ Cᴀᴍᴘɢʀᴏᴜɴᴅ will be on
the left.
GPS coordinates: N 39 42.911' / W 84 15.857'
Other: Maps of this park show an Argonne Campground meant primarily for equestrians, but it no
longer exists.
About the campground: This park is one of two in the system (the other being Sugarcreek) that
has guaranteed water in the campsite.
Why it's worth a visit: Possum Creek MetroPark is an example of how nature can recover if just
given a chance. It was once farmland, but it was degraded over time; dumps cropped up to mar
the landscape. An effort to replant the area in native prairie grasslands and flowers was made
and succeeded. What's resulted is one of the largest and most diverse prairie habitats in Ohio.
It accounts for nearly 20 percent of the park's 500-plus acres. There's some restored farmland
to explore, too. Located in the park's extreme southern end, it's a working farm stocked with live
animals. Families can sign up for a "family chores program" to learn about farming, while kids
can enjoy the "Polly Possum" play area. There are trails to walk and ride, with several trails going
through the Argonne Forest, which contains remnants of an amusement park that once existed for
World War I veterans. And don't overlook the fishing. Argonne Lake is big enough for non-powered
craft and there are several other ponds. Catfish are stocked the first Fri of the month all summer in
the former, with trout provided periodically. No fishing license is required.

100 Germantown MetroPark

Location: West of Germantown
Season: Year-round
Sites: 2, for tents only, with Old Mill capable of holding 25 people, Shrimps Hollow 60
Maximum RV length: N/A
Facilities: Vault toilet, picnic tables, fire rings, water (seasonally), canoe launch
Fee per night: Free

A pair of tiger swallowtail butterflies at Germantown MetroPark.

Pets: Leashed pets permitted
Activities: Canoeing and kayaking, fishing, hiking, sledding, backpacking, fossil collecting
Management: Five Rivers MetroParks
Contact: For reservations call (937) 277-4374; www.metroparks.org/Parks/Germantown/Home
.aspx.
Finding the campground: From Germantown, head west on SR 725/Market Street for 1.3 miles.
Turn right onto Creek Road, go 1 mile, take a slight left to stay on Creek and go another 0.4 mile.
Continue straight as Creek Road becomes Conservancy Road. At the next intersection make a
sharp right onto Old Mil Road and follow signs to CAMPGROUND.
GPS coordinates: N 39 38.444' / W 84 23.991'
Other: Twin Valley Backpacking Trail also runs through this park. It stretches 22 miles, winding
through woods that are cut by countless streams. The trail's Oak Ridge Backcountry Campsite is
here.
About the campground: Old Mill Campground is in the Bob Seibenthaler Natural Area, which is
especially pretty in spring, when the many wildflowers are in bloom. Shrimps Hollow Group Camp
is located on the park's eastern edge.
Why it's worth a visit: If your tastes in parks run toward the wild and untamed, this nearly 1,700-
acre park is the one for you. It's not wilderness. But it is a relatively large, significant assortment
of habitat types. There are steep hillsides, creek bottoms, wetlands, old-growth forest, ponds,
grasslands, and cedar glades. That mixture produces some plants and animals not found elsewhere locally. The old growth, fittingly accessible only by walking several miles and crossing several
streams, is especially pretty when spring's wildflowers are in bloom. Be sure to look for the numerous species of small orchids in particular. A shorter walk worth taking is the one that leads to
Valley Overlook. It offers a very nice view of Twin Valley Creek. Germantown also houses a nature
center that's largely underground. That makes it environmentally friendly. It's got a lot of hands-on
exhibits that really appeal to kids and a 500-foot wheelchair-accessible boardwalk.

101 Twin Creek MetroPark

Location: South of Germantown
Season: Year-round
Sites: 3, for tents only, capable of holding 25 to 35 people each
Maximum RV length: N/A
Facilities: Vault toilet, picnic tables, fire rings, water (seasonally), "natuary," lodge, amphitheater, fishing pier
Fee per night: Free
Pets: Leashed pets permitted
Activities: Hiking, canoeing and kayaking, horseback riding, fishing
Management: Five Rivers MetroParks
Contact: For reservations call (937) 277-4374; www.metroparks.org/Parks/TwinCreek/Home.aspx.
Finding the campground: From Germantown, head south on South Main Street, continuing straight for 1.6 miles after it becomes Eby Road, then another 0.4 mile after that becomes Franklin-Madison Road. Turn left onto Chamberlain Road and go 0.9 mile. Take the first right onto Morningstar Drive and go a little more than a mile. The entrance to the campground will be on the right.
GPS coordinates: N 39 34.726' / W 84 21.073'
Other: This park also has a backcountry site for backpackers. It's known as the Pine Ridge Camp.
About the campground: This park has three campsites, numbered 1, 2, and 3, that going forward are also going to be known by the names given them by the Boy Scouts decades ago: Tecumseh, Geronimo, and Little Turtle respectively.
Why it's worth a visit: There's a lot to see at Twin Creek MetroPark. Some of it, though, requires a knowing eye. Park at the Eby Road parking lot and you get a scenic view of Germantown, Carlisle, and Miamisburg. Some interesting wildlife, like northern harriers, bobolinks, and grasshopper sparrows, are common on the ridgetop, so you may spot them fairly easily. Farther south in the park, and accessible by walking the 1.6 mile green trail, is what's known as the Hopewell Earthwork. It's a long, winding mound of raised earth 3 to 4 feet tall constructed 2,000 years ago by the Hopewell tribe. It's known as Carlisle Fort and is on the National Register of Historic Places. It would have stood out on the landscape then; today it's largely hidden by forest. Information available in the park tells you where it is and how to look for it, though. While in the park, spend some time on and near Twin Creek. It's floatable in canoes and kayaks, and popular with fishermen. The reason? It's one of the cleanest, highest-quality streams in all of Ohio, rich in bug and other aquatic life. Combine that with the solitude you can often enjoy at this 1,000-acre park and it's a real treasure. The park also contains the Twin Valley Backpacking Trail, two ponds where you can cast a line without first buying a license and some nice horseback riding trails.

102 Sugarcreek MetroPark

Location: South of Bellbrook
Season: Year-round
Sites: 2, for tents only, each capable of holding 35 people
Maximum RV length: N/A
Facilities: Vault toilet, picnic tables, fire rings, nature play area, water
Fee per night: Free
Pets: Leashed pets permitted
Activities: Hiking, horseback riding, fishing, cross-country skiing, birding
Management: Five Rivers MetroParks
Contact: For reservations call (937) 277-4374; www.metroparks.org/Parks/SugarCreek/Home.aspx.
Finding the campground: From Bellbrook, follow South Main Street for 0.4 mile, continuing straight for another 0.1 mile when South Main becomes Waynesville Road. Turn right onto Ferry Road and go 1.4 miles. Turn left onto Conference Road and go to the park entrance, on the right, to reach Ash Campground; continue straight on Ferry to reach Oak Campground, which will be on the left.
GPS coordinates: N 39 37.344' / W 84 05.507' for Ash Campground; N 39 37.377' / W 84 05.447' for Oak Campground
Other: If you want to see something unusual here, explore the park's Sycamore Ridge. Sycamores are usually a tree of stream bottoms and creek edges. Here, though, they grow in profusion on a ridgetop. That suggests a shallow underground water source.
About the campground: Ash Campground is close to the park's main day-use area; Oak Campground sits off by itself on the park's eastern edge.
Why it's worth a visit: Sugarcreek is a simple but interesting park. It does not have a lot of "attractions" per se: no farm, no nature center, no horseback riding lessons. But it's a pleasure to visit. There's fishing in Sugar Creek and a variety of hiking trails that lead to some interesting natural features. One not to be missed is the "Three Sisters" cluster of oak trees. The sisters are three oak trees that started growing in 1440. They won't last forever; already there are signs of decline. But they still exist and, at just 0.7 mile from the parking lot, are worth the little bit of time it takes to find them. Not too much farther away on the same orange trail is the "Osage Orange Tunnel." It's a natural tunnel formed by the overarching branches of ancient Osage orange trees. They were originally planted in the late 1800s to create a fencerow. Elsewhere in the park you'll find a planted prairie. It contains wildflowers and plants reminiscent of Ohio's past, when prairie habitats were common and widespread. One of the best times to explore it is mid to late summer, when flowering plants that can reach more than 10 feet tall are in bloom.

Northwest

If you've ever wanted to camp on an island so big that people actually live on it, this is the place to visit.

Northwest Ohio has not one but three state parks that offer camping on islands in Lake Erie. A couple of other parks nearby, like East Harbor State Park, offer camping right on the lake shore. Crowds like those seen nowhere else in Ohio flock to them. You won't find solitude—one of the islands, South Bass, is home to a party town called the "Key West of Lake Erie"—but the tradeoff is an experience unlike any other.

There are some quieter places, too. Van Buren State Park is small but peaceful, a favorite of horseback riders looking to explore forested trails. Mary Jane Thurston State Park is likewise a gentle park. You'll hear some traffic, but it offers a small, hidden campground where you can otherwise relax and fish. And Lake Loramie? Its fields of floating lotus are beautiful. To see the dinner plate-sized flowers in bloom in some of its quiet bays, standing tall above the water and surrounded by pads as flat and wide as serving trays, is a treat.

This is also the place to come experience a watery scavenger hunt. Here you can explore an old panel truck, an abandoned police cruiser, a forest of seahorse statues, and even an enchanted forest. The kicker is that all of those things are under water in a lake so clear you can see to depths of more than a dozen feet. White Star Park offers scuba diving so good it's considered one of the premier inland sites in the entire state.

When you're ready for something else, this corner of the state is home to Cedar Point, an amusement park that boasts two of the tallest and fastest roller coasters in the country. If you feel the need to plunge 400 feet at 120 miles an hour, pay the park a visit. The Armstrong Air and Space Museum can also be found locally, as can the Rutherford B. Hayes Presidential Center and the Merry-Go-Round Museum.

All in all, this is a great region for adventure. Pick the kind you want, or mix and match a couple, and go.

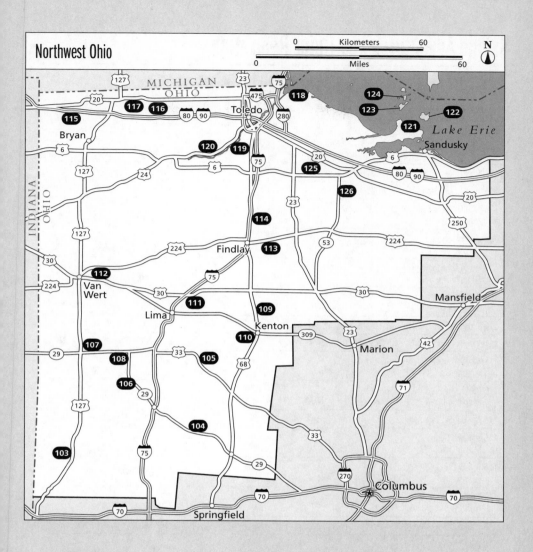

Island Adventures and Quiet Relaxation

	total sites	hookups	max RV lengths	toilets	showers	drinking water	dump station	recreation	fee	reservation
103 Darke County Fairgrounds	600	Y	N/A	F	Y	Y	Y	HC	$$$$	N
104 Kiser Lake State Park	118	Y	30	V	N	Y	Y	HBFSLU	$$$$	Y
105 Indian Lake State Park	452	Y	45	F	Y	Y	Y	HBFSLUEE	$$$$	Y
106 Lake Loramie State Park	175	Y	50	F	Y	Y	Y	HBFSLUEE	$$$$	Y
107 Mercer County Fairgrounds	155	Y	N/A	F	Y	Y	Y	HBFS	$-$$$$	Y
108 Grand Lake St. Marys State Park	204	Y	50	F	Y	Y	Y	BFSCLU	$$$$	Y
109 Hardin County Fairgrounds	110	Y	N/A	F	Y	Y	Y	N/A	$$	Y
110 Saulisberry Park	50	Y	30	F	Y	Y	Y	HBFCO	$$$-$$$$	Y
111 Ottawa Metro Park	30	Y	N/A	F	Y	Y	Y	HFBSCL	$$$$	N
112 Van Wert County Fairgrounds	800	Y	N/A	F	Y	Y	Y	N/A	$$$	Y
113 Riverbend Recreation Area	8	N	N/A	V	N	N	N	HBFREE	$	Y
114 Van Buren State Park	59	Y	50	V	N	Y	Y	HBFCLU	$$$$	Y
115 Williams County Fairgrounds	178	Y	N/A	F	Y	Y	Y	N/A	$$$$	N
116 Fulton County Fairgrounds	600	Y	N/A	F	Y	Y	Y	N/A	$$$$	Y
117 Harrison Lake State Park	173	Y	50	F	Y	Y	Y	HBFSLEE	$$$$	Y
118 Maumee Bay State Park	252	Y	50	F	Y	Y	Y	HBFSCLU	$$$$	Y
119 Buttonwood/Betty C. Black Recreation Area	15	N	N/A	V	N	N	N	FB	$	N
120 Mary Jane Thurston State Park	35	Y	40	V	N	Y	Y	HBFLUEE	$$$$	Y
121 East Harbor State Park	571	Y	40	F	Y	Y	Y	HBFSLUEE	$$$$	Y
122 Kelleys Island State Park	127	Y	50	F	Y	Y	Y	FBSLU	$$$$	Y
123 South Bass Island State Park	135	Y	45	F	Y	Y	Y	BFSL	$$$$	Y
124 Middle Bass Island State Park	21	N	N/A	V	N	N	N	BFC	$$$	Y
125 White Star Park	48	Y	88	V	N	Y	Y	HBFSCRU	$$$-$$$$	N
126 Wolf Creek Park	24	N	45	V	N	Y	N	HBFC	$$$	N

See fee codes on page xx and amenities codes on page xxiii.

103 Darke County Fairgrounds

Location: Northwest of Dayton
Season: Apr–Oct, excluding Aug when the fair is going on
Sites: 600
Maximum RV length: No restrictions
Facilities: Flush toilets, warm showers, water, electricity, sewer, sanitary dump station
Fee per night: $$$$
Pets: Permitted at some sites
Activities: Hiking, biking, museums nearby
Management: Darke County Agricultural Society
Contact: (937) 548-5044 or (800) 736-3671; http://darkecountyfair.com/camping.htm. Campsites are first come, first served, though groups should call in advance.
Finding the campground: From Dayton, follow I-75 north for 7.4 miles until you can get onto I-70 west. Go 10.3 miles, then merge onto SR 49 north toward Greenville via exit 24. Go 22 miles. The entrance to the campground will be on the left.
GPS coordinates: N 40 05.283' / W 84 38.156'
Other: Groups of ten or more are asked to call in advance to make sure that there are no activities going on at the fairgrounds that are limiting space.
About the campground: The sites offer a mix of shade and sun. Campers self-register upon arrival. Weekly and monthly rates are available for long-term campers.
Why it's worth a visit: This is a 185-acre facility with an awful lot of space for campers, with much of the grounds pleasantly wooded. It's also a reasonably priced place to stay while visiting Darke County's many attractions. This area of Ohio is big on antique shops and has several art galleries. It's also home to the KitchenAid Heritage Center, where you can explore the history of appliances and take cooking classes. Perhaps the most unique thing about the area is its attachment to Annie Oakley, the cowgirl sharpshooter of Buffalo Bill's Wild West Show. In downtown Greenville is Annie Oakley Memorial Park, with a life-size bronze statue and a historical marker that explains her exploits. To really find out about this diminutive star, though, check out the Garst Museum. It's home to exhibits and memorabilia about the woman who was America's first real female superstar. Details can be found at www.GarstMuseum.org.

104 Kiser Lake State Park

Location: Northwest of Urbana
Season: Apr–Dec
Sites: 118
Maximum RV length: 30 feet
Facilities: Vault toilets, electricity, sanitary dump station, water, picnic tables, fire rings, boat rental, boat launch, nature preserve
Fee per night: $$$$
Pets: Leashed pets permitted
Activities: Boating, fishing, hiking, swimming, hunting

A solitary water lily floats on the surface of Kiser Lake at Kiser Lake State Park.

Management: Ohio Department of Natural Resources
Contact: (937) 362-3822 park office, (937) 362-3565 campground; www.dnr.state.oh.us/parks/parks/kisrlake/tabid/751/Default.aspx. For reservations call (866) 644-6727 or visit www.ohio.reserveworld.com. Some sites are first come, first served.
Finding the campground: From Urbana, follow US 36 west for 6.7 miles. Take a slight right onto Zimmerman Road and go 3.7 miles, turn right onto Heck Road and then an almost immediate left onto Ward Road. Go 0.4 mile then take the second left onto Cemetery Road. Take the first left onto Ford Road, then another left onto Highway 64/Trestle Road. Turn right and follow Kiser Lake Road to the campground.
GPS coordinates: N 40 10.832' / W 83 56.979'
Other: This park has two organized group tenting areas; a camper cabin and an equestrian camp.
About the campground: This is a smaller campground, but with lots of privacy. Sites 71 to 78 are especially nice; sites 52 to 61 are the only ones with electricity.
Why it's worth a visit: There's nothing quite so colorful or intriguing as a sailboat, its bright flag stretched tight with wind, silently and effortlessly gliding across a lake. That's just what you'll see at clear, clean Kiser Lake. Motors are prohibited on this 396-acre lake, so it's a favorite with sailboaters as well as paddlers. Don't overlook opportunities to do some exploring on land, too. The park is home to the Kiser Lake Wetlands Nature Preserve, which exists in two tracts on the lake's south shore. Once a bog and now a mix of meadows, marsh and woods, it's a place where you can see such unusual wildflowers as big bluestem, queen of the prairie and Ohio goldenrod. Throughout the park, look for some of the many boulders deposited here by advancing and retreating glaciers.

105 Indian Lake State Park

Location: East of Wapakoneta
Season: Mid-Apr–Oct
Sites: 452
Maximum RV length: 45 feet
Facilities: Flush toilets, warm showers, electricity, water, picnic tables, fire rings, laundry facility, camp commissary, boat launch, docks and rental, environmental education programs, playgrounds, miniature golf course, basketball and volleyball courts, bike rental, games and sporting equipment available to loan for campers
Fee per night: $$$$
Pets: Permitted on some sites
Activities: Fishing, hiking, boating, hunting, swimming, golfing
Management: Ohio Department of Natural Resources
Contact: (937) 843-2717 park office, (937) 843-3553 campground office; www.dnr.state.oh.us/parks/parks/indianlk/tabid/746/Default.aspx. For reservations call (866) 644-6727 or visit www.ohio.reserveworld.com.
Finding the campground: From Wapakoneta, head east on US 33 for 12.7 miles. Stay straight to go on SR 385 for 6.3 miles, then turn right onto SR 385/117 for about 2 miles. Turn right onto SR 235 and follow the signs to CAMPGROUND.
GPS coordinates: N 40 31.120' / W 83 54.003'
Other: This park has an organized group tenting area and rents three camper cabins.
About the campground: This campground is divided into three sections—1, 2, and 3—and they vary in whether they offer electricity only or full-service hookups. All are similar in that they have a lot of sites crammed tightly together. Some services, such as electricity, are unavailable during the off-season.
Why it's worth a visit: People have been coming to Indian Lake for a long time. At the start of the twentieth century it was a resort known as the "Midwest's Million Dollar Playground." Today it's still very popular, with the huge waterway that is Indian Lake still the draw. It covers 5,800 acres, meaning there are more than 7 acres of water for every one acre of land at the park. Campers and day users come to water ski, fish, and swim. That latter activity can be done at the park's two public beaches and at three areas where you can swim off your boat: at Walnut Islands, Red Oak Island, and Oldfield Beach. There's some wonderful wildlife viewing available, too. The park lies along one of the nation's major aviation routes, so in fall and spring especially it's common to see large numbers of Canada geese, ducks, swans, egrets, and herons. If that doesn't do it for you, there are three trails to explore, with the 1-mile Pew Island Trail especially worth the effort for the views it offers. Cyclists can use a BMX track.

106 Lake Loramie State Park

Location: East of Fort Loramie
Season: Apr–Dec
Sites: 175, some walk-in only

A watery field of Lotus flowers fill one of the bays at Lake Loramie State Park.

Maximum RV length: 50 feet

Facilities: Flush toilets, warm showers, water, electricity, sanitary dump station, picnic tables, fire rings, miniature golf course, free WiFi for registered campers, boat launches and tie-ups, environmental education programs, canoe rental

Fee per night: $$$$

Pets: Leashed pets permitted

Activities: Fishing, hiking, boating, swimming, hunting, golfing

Management: Ohio Department of Natural Resources

Contact: (937) 295-2011 park office, (937) 295-3900 campground; www.dnr.state.oh.us/parks/parks/lakeloramie/tabid/758/Default.aspx. For reservations call (866) 644-6727 or visit www.ohio.reserveworld.com. Some sites are first come, first served.

Finding the campground: From Fort Loramie, go northeast on SR 66 for about 0.1 mile, then take the first right onto SR 362. Go 1.1 miles and turn left to stay on SR 362. And follow the signs to CAMPGROUND.

GPS coordinates: N 40 21.394' / W 84 21.428'

Other: This park rents three cedar cabins and four rent-a-camp sites and has two areas for organized group tenting.

About the campground: The non-electric, non-reservable sites actually have the most room and are closest to the footbridge leading to Lakeview Trail. Sites 20 to 39 are the premium lakeview sites and closest to the canoe rental.

Why it's worth a visit: This is a big 1,650-acre lake with no horsepower limits, but—unlike many waters this size—no waterskiing is permitted. In fact, save for one designated speed zone on the lake's western end, the whole thing is managed under "no-wake" rules. That makes for some interesting opportunities. You can fish for common species like crappies and bluegills using just about any size boat you want without having to worry about competition from people for whom speed is the thing. Paddlers can also explore the lake's many, many coves and fingers and check out its water lilies, cattails, and American lotus without being bounced around. Equally interesting are some of the natural features to be seen from land. There are several trails, but the one leading to Blackberry Island is especially good in that it sometimes offers glimpses of nesting barred owls and red-headed woodpeckers. Keep an eye out for the bald Cyprus trees and sweet gum growing within the campground, too.

107 Mercer County Fairgrounds

Location: West of Wapokeneta
Season: Apr–Oct, excluding fair week
Sites: 155
Maximum RV length: No restriction
Facilities: Showers, flush toilets, electricity, water, sanitary dump station, picnic tables, horseshoe pits
Fee per night: $ to $$$$
Pets: Leashed pets permitted
Activities: Swimming, fishing, boating, hiking nearby
Management: Mercer County Agricultural Society
Contact: For reservations call (419) 586-3239; www.mercercountyohiofair.com/Camping-Info .html. Self-registration is available during off hours.
Finding the campground: From Wapokeneta, head west on US 33 for 9.9 miles. Continue another 8.5 miles after US 33 becomes SR 29 west. Stay straight to go on West Market Street, continuing for another 0.9 mile to the fairground entrance. Follow the signs to Campground.
GPS coordinates: N 40 33.059' / W 84 34.988'
Other: Fires are permitted in designated areas, but only for cooking purposes.
About the campground: Campers can stay long term, with monthly rates available.
Why it's worth a visit: This campground is located adjacent to Grand Lake St. Marys State Park, so you can camp here inexpensively and take advantage of all that's available at the park. There's a lot to do within Mercer County itself, too. There are a number of interesting museums. The Armstrong Air and Space Museum in Wapokeneta—named for Neil Armstrong, the first man to walk on the moon—is one. It chronicles Ohio's contributions to America's space program. Fort Recovery State Museum pays tribute to two battles that paved the way for the opening of the frontier. There are hands-on exhibits, artifacts explaining Native American history and trails. Then there's the Bicycle Museum of America, which has more than 300 cycles, ranging from one built in 1816 to those used by the US Army infantry in World War I to the bike from the movie *Pee-wee's Big Adventure*.

108 Grand Lake St. Marys State Park

Location: West of Wapakoneta

Season: Apr–Dec

Sites: 204

Maximum RV length: 50 feet

Facilities: Flush toilets, warm showers, electricity, sanitary dump station, water, picnic tables, fire rings, laundry facility, camp store, free WiFi for registered campers, boat launch and tie-ups, seasonal environmental education programs, games, fishing gear and sporting equipment available to loan for campers, bike rentals, miniature golf course, playground, basketball and volleyball courts and horseshoe pits, dog park

Fee per night: $$$$

Pets: Permitted in some areas

Activities: Swimming, biking, fishing, hunting, boating, golfing

Management: Ohio Department of Natural Resources

Contact: (419) 394-3611 park office, (419) 394-2774 campground office; www.dnr.state.oh .us/parks/parks/grndlake/tabid/737/Default.aspx. For reservations call (866) 644-6727 or visit www.ohio.reserveworld.com.

Finding the campground: From Wapakoneta, head west on US 33 for 6.7 miles. Merge onto SR 66 south for 1.6 miles, then turn East Spring Street/SR 29 west and go 0.3 mile. Take the third right onto North Front Street/SR 29 west, go 0.4 mile, turn left onto North Wayne Street, go about 500 feet, and take the first right onto Jackson Street/SR 703. Go until you can turn onto SR 364 north. Turn left onto Edgewater Drive to enter the campground.

GPS coordinates: N 40 32.828' / W 84 26.257'

Other: This park has an organized group tenting area as well as five camper cabins and two cedar cabins. As of 2012, this park was offering a 25 percent discount on all camping and dock fees, perhaps because algae toxins in the lake had the park warning the very young, very old, and those with weak immune systems to avoid swimming or wading in the lake.

About the campground: This is another large, tightly packed campground. Sites 208 to 217 are the most secluded, but they are also non-electric.

Why it's worth a visit: Grand Lake St. Marys was for a long while known as the largest man-made impoundment in the world. It covers 13,500 acres, having been built originally as a feeder reservoir for the Miami-Erie Canal. The park remains one of the oldest in Ohio's state system. Visitors can boat—there are no horsepower restrictions on the lake—and fish for a variety of warmwater and coolwater species, from bass to yellow perch. A lot of duck hunting goes on here, too. The park has seventy seasonal duck blinds that are awarded by lottery. Surprisingly, there is not much in the way of developed hiking trails, despite the fact that the lake has 52 miles of shoreline. But there are paths for cross-country skiers and snowmobilers that can be walked in the warmer months. You can also check out a state-run fish hatchery on the lake's eastern shore.

109 Hardin County Fairgrounds

Location: East of Lima

Season: Year-round

Sites: 110

Maximum RV length: No restrictions

Facilities: Flush toilets, showers, water, electricity, sanitary dump station

Fee per night: $$

Pets: Leashed pets permitted

Activities: Activities on site, nearby attractions

Management: Hardin County Agricultural Society

Contact: www.hardincountyfair.org/; for reservations call (419) 675-2396 9 a.m. to 4 p.m. Wed and Fri; otherwise, sites are available on a first come, first served basis by seeing the grounds-keeper when you arrive.

Finding the campground: From I-75 in Lima, head east on SR 117/309/Harding Highway for about 26.4 miles. Turn right onto SR 67/68 and go 1.1 miles to the fairgrounds. Follow the signs to Camping Area.

GPS coordinates: N 40 38.072' / W 83 36.697'

Other: The only time camping is not permitted here is the week to ten days immediately preceding the county fair and the week to ten days immediately after it. It's held each year from Tue through Sun after Labor Day.

About the campground: The sites here are all in open sun.

Why it's worth a visit: If you time your visit right, you can combine a stay at the fairgrounds with a visit to the annual Gene Autry Days festival. Held on the fairgrounds, the celebration of all things cowboy related has been going on for about twenty years. It features entertainers, fast draw competitions, antique and western toys and collectibles, cap guns, and lots of food. It's held each year in late June. Details are available from the Hardin County Chamber and Business Alliance at (419) 673-4131 or www.hardinohio.org/new/Tourism.aspx. Located very near the fairgrounds is the Historic Village and Farm, a collection of old buildings—a schoolhouse, railroad station, log cabin, and jail—that date from 1861 to 1893. Visitors to the museum can see woodworking tools, antique farm machinery, a working weaver's loom and more. It's open by appointment from May through September. Visit www.hardinmuseums.org or call (419) 673-7147. While here you might also want to check out Lawrence Woods State Nature Preserve. It encompasses nearly 1,100 acres. What makes it special is its mature forest, which is unlike just about anything else in this region. Its uniqueness makes it home to a variety of otherwise locally rare plants and animals. This is one of only three places in Ohio where heart-leaf plantain is known to occur, for example. More common species here are white, yellow, red and bur oaks, beech, white ash, shagbark hickory, sugar maple, and sycamore. This park is also popular for viewing wildflowers in spring and birds year-round. Information and directions are available at http://ohiodnr.com/dnap/location/lawrence_woods/tabid/905/Default.aspx.

110 Saulisberry Park

Location: East of Lima
Season: Apr 1–Oct 31
Sites: 50
Maximum RV length: 30 feet
Facilities: Showers, flush toilets, water, electricity, sanitary dump station fire rings, playground, boat docks, boat launch, basketball courts
Fee per night: $$$ to $$$$
Pets: Leashed pets permitted
Activities: Fishing, boating with electric motors only, hiking, mountain biking, off-road dirt biking
Management: City of Kenton
Contact: For reservations call (419) 675-4850; www.kentoncity.com/Parks/parks.htm.
Finding the campground: From Lima, head east on SR 309/117/Harding Highway for 18.8 miles. Turn right onto CR 95 and go 4.2 miles. Stay straight and continue another 2.8 miles after CR 95 becomes Binghman Road. Turn left onto SR 67 and go about 4 miles until you see signs for Saulisberry Park on the right. Follow the gravel road to the campground.
GPS coordinates: N 40 37.089' / W 83 38.095'
Other: Seasonal passes are available for campers with RVs and tents
About the campground: The sites here, thirty-four of which offer amenities, are a mix of sun and shade.
Why it's worth a visit: This park occupies land that once was a stone quarry. When operations ceased, the roughly 200-acre site was donated to the City of Kenton and became Saulisberry Park. It opened to the public in about 1970. Visitors can find a lot to do. France Lake is not big at about 10 acres, but it's full of bass, bluegills, crappies, channel catfish, and carp. A number of fishing derbies are held on it throughout the year. It's open to paddlers and boaters using trolling motors. You don't need a fishing license or a boat registration to use it, but you do have to purchase a fishing and/or boating pass. The former is $10 annually, the latter $20. Hikers and bikers will find wooded trails and paved multi-use pathways. Fans of dirt bikes can do their thing here, too, so long as their equipment meets state standards. Riders are urged to stick to designated trails. There's plenty of open space for kids to play games and picnic. The park seems on the upswing, with the city devoting more attention and money to it in recent years.

111 Ottawa Metro Park Campground

Location: East of Lima
Season: Mid-Apr–mid-Oct
Sites: 30, 3 of them ADA accessible
Maximum RV length: No limits
Facilities: Flush toilets, warm showers, water, electricity, sanitary dump station, picnic tables, fire rings, vending machines, amphitheater, volleyball court, boat launch, horseshoe pits
Fee per night: $$$$
Pets: Leashed pets permitted

Robert E. Lee Sweetgum
Liquidambar styraciflua

The Robert E. Lee Sweetgum grows at Stratford Hall, the Virginia plantation where the famous Confederate general was born. In 1865, during the Civil War, Lee became Supreme Commander of all the Confederate armies. Long respected and honored by Southerners, Lee has also been considered a hero by all Americans.

Pioneers used the gum, or resin, obtained from the inner bark of this tree for medicinal purposes and chewing gum. Ohio is located at the northern edge of the sweetgum's range, which extends as far south as Central America.

Visitors to Ottawa MetroPark can learn about trees by walking the paved trail through its arboretum.

Activities: Hiking, fishing, boating, swimming, disc golf, biking

Management: Johnny Appleseed Metropolitan Park District

Contact: (419) 221-1232; www.jampd.com/things-to-do!/camping.aspx. No reservations are taken; it's first come, first served.

Finding the campground: From Lima, head east on SR 81 for about 3 miles. The park entrance will be on your right. Signs within the park will direct you to the campground.

GPS coordinates: N 40 45.310' / W 84 03.429'

Other: There are eight pull-through sites for campers with exceptionally large RVs.

About the campground: The sites here are all in full sun, in a well-manicured, neat, well-laid-out campground.

Why it's worth a visit: This park in Allen County is a very nice multi-use facility. It only takes in a bit over 287 acres, but there's a 450-foot swimming beach with a 10-foot inflatable water slide for kids, as well as a "raindrop" water fountain. "Family Fun Days" at the beach that feature special events are scheduled when school's out. There are a couple of playgrounds, too, and a beach house and changing station. An amphitheater hosts special programs every Sat night throughout summer. Away from the beach is a separate lake, Lake Lima. It's 89 acres and is open to fishing—though shore access is not the best—and boating, with nonpowered craft and those with electric motors allowed. You can also hike. There's a paved path throughout the park that winds through fields and woods. A unique feature is the signs that reference tree species. The signs note how each tree, like the Robert E. Lee Sweetgum, is connected to a specific historic place where it grows, such as Lee's Stratford Hall Plantation. Some details on what the trees are used for is also provided. A flier available from the parks district explains it all.

112 Van Wert County Fairgrounds

Location: South of Paulding

Season: Apr 1–Nov 15

Sites: 800

Maximum RV length: No restriction

Facilities: Showers, flush toilets, water, electricity, sanitary dump station, WiFi for an additional fee

Fee per night: $$$

Pets: Leashed pets permitted

Activities: Various events held on the grounds throughout the year

Management: Van Wert Agricultural Society

Contact: For reservations call (419) 238-9270; www.vanwertcountyfair.com/index.htm.

Finding the campground: From Paulding, head south on US 127 for 16.6 miles. Turn right onto US 127/SR 224 and continue following 127 for 3.4 miles. The fairgrounds will be on the right; follow the signs to FAIR OFFICE.

GPS coordinates: N 40 51.412' / W 84 35.091'

Other: This fairgrounds specializes in hosting RV rallies and can accommodate up to 1,200 units.

About the campground: Most of the sites are in grassy areas, but there are a few that offer more shade. The fairgrounds is a member of a couple of discount RV park programs.

Why it's worth a visit: Like most fairgrounds, this one can serve as a base camp for exploring the surrounding area. You can also tie a visit to several interesting events right on the grounds. The Van Wert County Historical Museum holds an annual Railroad Heritage Weekend in July focusing on model trains. There are railroad-related entertainment and demonstrations and refreshments. Often on that same weekend the Van Wert Amateur Radio Club holds its "Hamfest," a celebration of shortwave radio. You can see electronics, radio gear, computers and software, and view demonstrations on how it all works. Perhaps the biggest event outside of the fair is the annual Apple Festival. Held in Oct, it draws thousands of people. They come for the crafts, wagon rides, entertainment and kids games, and most of all for the apples. There's cider, pie, dumplings, and butter, along with all kinds of other food.

113 Riverbend Recreation Area

Location: East of Findlay
Season: Year-round
Sites: 8, though groups of up to 100 people can stay with prior approval
Maximum RV length: N/A
Facilities: Vault toilets, picnic tables, fire rings, dog park, disc golf course, playground, interpretive and activity centers, boathouse, launch ramp, volleyball courts
Fee per night: $
Pets: Leashed pets permitted
Activities: Hiking, horseback riding, fishing, boating, cross-country skiing, snowshoeing, environmental education programs
Management: Hancock Parks District
Contact: www.hancockparks.com/YourParks/RiverbendRecreationArea.aspx. For reservations call (419) 425-7275.
Finding the campground: From Findlay, head east on SR 568 for 4.5 miles. Turn right onto TH 241 and go 0.2 mile. Turn right onto TH 208 and follow the signs to Campground.
GPS coordinates: N 41 01.940' / W 83 33.643'
Other: This is Hancock County's first park. It opened in 1976. It sits on what is believed to have been a Native American campsite for years.
About the campground: Campers need to bring their own firewood to this campground, which is open to tents only.
Why it's worth a visit: None of the trails in Riverbend Recreation Area are especially long. The bridle trail, at a bit less than 2 miles, is the longest. But all follow the Blanchard River and offer nice scenery and the chance to see waterbirds. You can also get information on the natural history of the area via panels in the Meadows and Big Oaks activity areas. The nearby Findlay Reservoir adds additional opportunities. Located adjacent to Riverbend Park and essentially considered a part of the recreation area, Reservoir #1 is 187 acres, while #2 is 640 acres. You can put a boat on the larger of the two. Both can be fished, and there are trails across the top of the dikes that are especially scenic at dawn and dusk. Mile markers along the way let you keep track of how far you've gone. The 20-mile Heritage Trail passes through Riverbend and around the reservoirs, too. In fall, hayrides are offered so visitors can see the fall colors.

This is a look toward one of the disc golf "holes" through another at Van Buren State Park.

114 Van Buren State Park

Location: North of Findlay
Season: May–early Dec
Sites: 59
Maximum RV length: 50 feet
Facilities: Vault toilets, electricity, picnic tables, sanitary dump station, fire rings, water, playground, amphitheater, games and sporting equipment available to loan for campers, disc golf course, boat launch
Fee per night: $$$$
Pets: Permitted at some sites
Activities: Hunting, hiking, biking, fishing, boating, disc golfing
Management: Ohio Department of Natural Resources
Contact: (419) 832-7662; www.dnr.state.oh.us/parks/parks/vanburen/tabid/794/Default.aspx. For reservations call (866) 644-6727 or visit www.ohio.reserveworld.com.
Finding the campground: From Findlay, head north on I-75 toward Toledo for 7.5 miles. Take exit 164 toward McComb/Fostoria and go right into SR 613 East for 0.7 mile. Turn right onto TH 218 and go past the park office until you come to the campground entrance on your right.
GPS coordinates: N 41 08.280' / W 83 37.156'
Other: If you don't have reservations, a self-registration station is located at the entrance to the campground. There's also an organized group tenting area and two camper cabins here.
About the campground: This campground has two loops. The first, camping area 1, is a family camp. The second, camping area 2, is the multi-use and equestrian camp. Tie rails, picket lines, and manure bins are available at designated sites. This equestrian camp with thirty sites is the only one of its kind in northwest Ohio.
Why it's worth a visit: This is a lovely little park in northwestern Ohio, a 251-acre patch of woods surrounded by rolling farm country. It's a peaceful place to get away. Its lake—open to electric motors only and non-powered craft—offers some decent fishing and some very nice flatwater paddling. There are calm days when dipping your paddle into the water is like splitting a piece of glass. More than anything, though, this park attracts people looking to explore its woods. Van Buren is particularly popular with horseback riders, who have their own campground. It leads directly to four bridle trails meandering around and through the park's eastern end. Hikers have five trails to choose from, with 3-mile Lakeshore Trail worthwhile if you want to access fishing spots, look for waterbirds, frogs and other wildlife and/or just take in the scenery. A blue-blazed single track mountain bike trail offers some challenges to those who like to pedal.

115 Williams County Fairgrounds

Location: West of Toledo
Season: May–Oct
Sites: 178
Maximum RV length: No restrictions

Facilities: Showers and flush toilets in the center of the fairgrounds, vault toilets in the campground, electricity, water, sanitary dump station, picnic tables, fire rings
Fee per night: $$$$
Pets: Leashed pets permitted
Activities: County fair, other activities on the grounds, nearby attractions
Management: Williams County Agricultural Society
Contact: (419) 485-3755; www.wcofair.com/index.html. No reservations are taken outside of fair week; it's first come, first served.
Finding the campground: From Toledo, follow SR 2 west for 4 miles, then turn left onto South Reynolds Road and go 1.7 miles, until you can merge onto I-80/I-90 west. Go 46.4 miles. Take exit 13 for SR 15, go 0.7 mile, and keep left at the fork to merge onto SR 15/US 20 Alternate east. Go 2 miles and turn right onto SR 107 west to reach the campground entrance. Follow the signs to CAMPING AREA.
GPS coordinates: N 41 35.355' / W 84 35.940'
Other: The fairgrounds is very near the Ohio Turnpike, so it's convenient for travelers.
About the campground: All of the sites here are pretty much in the open sun.
Why it's worth a visit: The Williams County Fair is one of the largest in the tri-state area, with demolition derbies, big-name headliner entertainment and all of the usual food, animals and crafts. It's held the week after Labor Day. Staying here allows you to visit some other interesting attractions, too. The Williams County Historical Society has a museum and several vintage log buildings. The Parkerburg Wildlife Area is nearby as well. It's 153 acres of grasslands and woods split by Beaver Creek, with two ponds. People come here to bird. The mating displays of woodcock are an especially neat treat in the meadows. Hunters pursue rabbits, ring-necked pheasants, and fox squirrels, along with deer, while fishermen chase largemouth bass, bluegills, and bullhead catfish. There are wineries and glass blowing businesses in the area, too.

116 Fulton County Fairgrounds

Location: North of Wauseon
Season: Year-round, but with facilities only Apr–Oct
Sites: 600
Maximum RV length: No restrictions
Facilities: Flush toilets, showers, water, electricity, sanitary dump station
Fee per night: $$$$
Pets: Leashed pets permitted
Activities: Various events on site and attractions nearby
Management: Fulton County Fair
Contact: For reservations call (419) 335-6006; www.fultoncountyfair.com.
Finding the campground: From Wauseon, head north on SR 108 for 1.6 miles. Turn left onto Alternate US 20/SR 108 and go 0.7 mile, then turn right onto SR 108 and go 1.5 miles to the fairground entrance and the campground.
GPS coordinates: N 41 35.825' / W 84 08.915'
Other: The annual fair is held around Labor Day each year.
About the campground: There are some trees, but the sites here are mostly in the open sun.

Why it's worth a visit: Like most fairgrounds, this one hosts a number of events throughout the year, from tractor pulls to gem shows. But one of its more unique attractions is the Midwest Geobash, billed as one of the world's largest annual geocaching events. It's a free four-day affair focused on geocaching: how to do it, where to do it, stories about it and more. The fairgrounds serve as the event's permanent site. Details are available at http://midwestgeobash.org. From here you can also visit all of Toledo's attractions. The Mud Hens are one. A minor league affiliate of Major League Baseball's Detroit Tigers, the team plays from Apr through early fall. Games are fun in their own right and, in keeping with minor league tradition, they're big on promotions, give-aways, and fun for families and children. Cedar Point amusement park is nearby, as is the Toledo Zoo, rated among the top 10 in the country. Sauder Village and Fort Meigs offer glimpses into the area's past, and the Toledo Speedway is a short-track venue.

117 Harrison Lake State Park

Location: West of Wauseon
Season: Apr–Dec
Sites: 173
Maximum RV length: 50 feet
Facilities: Flush toilets, warm showers, water, sanitary dump station, electricity, picnic tables, fire rings, playground, games and sporting equipment available to loan for campers, boat launch, environmental education programs
Fee per night: $$$$
Pets: Permitted at some sites
Activities: Boating, fishing, swimming, hiking
Management: Ohio Department of Natural Resources
Contact: (419) 237-2593; www.dnr.state.oh.us/parks/parks/harrison/tabid/740/Default.aspx. For reservations call (866) 644-6727 or visit www.ohio.reserveworld.com.
Finding the campground: From Wauseon, head west north on SR 108 for 1.6 miles. Turn left onto Alternate US 20 west and go 10 miles, then turn right onto SR 66 and go 4.1 miles. Turn left onto CR M, go about 1.6 miles, then follow the signs for Campground.
GPS coordinates: N 41 38.656' / W 84 22.030' for area 1; N 41 38.243' / W 84 21.819' for areas 2 and 3
Other: This park also rents one camper cabin and two yurts.
About the campground: This campground is broken into three areas—1, 2 and 3—with one the largest and three the smallest. Area 1 is on Harrison Lake's north shore and all of its sites are electric; areas 2 and 3 are on the lake's south shore, with some of the sites in area 2 and none of those in 3 having electricity.
Why it's worth a visit: This park is an oasis, not in that it's an island of green in a desert, but in that it's an island of woods in a land of acre upon acre of corn, soybeans, and other farm products. It's small at 142 acres. But there's fun to be had. The park has a lake for boating, swimming, and fishing, with everything from largemouth and smallmouth bass to northern pike and crappies to be caught. There's even a section of lake set aside for swimming with your dog. Be sure if you visit to hike the 3.5-mile trail that circles the lake. It not only provides some good access for shore fishing, but is often a gateway for seeing some of the park's wildlife. The lake's

shallow western end commonly hosts great blue herons and egrets, frogs, snakes, and dragon-flies. In the woods you can sometimes see box turtles, red foxes, and the otherwise uncommon thirteen-lined ground squirrel.

118 Maumee Bay State Park

Location: East of Toledo
Season: May–Dec
Sites: 252
Maximum RV length: 50 feet
Facilities: Flush toilets, warm showers, water, electricity, sanitary dump station, boat launch, picnic tables, fire rings, playground, basketball court, horseshoe pits, bike rental, games and sporting equipment available to loan for campers, nature center, golf course
Fee per night: $$$$
Pets: Permitted at all sites
Activities: Biking, hiking, fishing, boating, swimming, golf, hunting
Management: Ohio Department of Natural Resources
Contact: (419) 836-7758 park office, (419) 836-8828 camp office (seasonal); www.dnr.state.oh.us/parks/parks/maumeebay/tabid/764/Default.aspx. For reservations call (866) 644-6727 or visit www.ohio.reserveworld.com.
Finding the campground: From Toledo, follow Consaul Street/Nancy Packo's Way for 1.3 miles. Continue another 5 miles as Consaul becomes Corduroy Street, then turn left onto North Norden Road and follow signs to CAMPGROUND.
GPS coordinates: N 41 40.644' / W 83 23.431'
Other: This park also has a 120-room lodge and conference center, twenty-four deluxe cottages and three rent-a-camp units.
About the campground: As a general rule, the sites within this campground are pretty tightly packed together. If you want a wee more space, try to get one of the spots located on the outside edge of the circular loops at the end of each road. On a map they look like flowers atop so many stems.
Why it's worth a visit: Located on the shores of Lake Erie, this is an interesting place to camp because of its wetlands. As a habitat type, wetlands hold a richer diversity of fish, reptiles, amphibians, birds, and mammals than any other. That certainly seems to be the case here, where more than 300 species of birds alone have been recorded. You might see anything from distinctive pintail ducks to killdeer and bald eagles. A couple of trails take you to all that. The easy 2-mile boardwalk is an especially good bet, given its interpretive signs and wheelchair access. A visit to the park's nature center beforehand is worthwhile so that you know what to look for. Of course, no mention of any park on Lake Erie is complete without talking about the fishing, and Maumee Bay offers access to terrific walleye angling. There are a couple of ponds within the campground open only to registered campers, too, as well as a pond near the lodge. Maumee Bay is also home to a "Scottish links" style 18-hole course that challenges golfers who must confront wind and other elements.

A gull sets its wings to land at Maumee Bay State Park.

119 Buttonwood/Betty C. Black Recreation Area

Location: Southwest of Toledo
Season: Mar–Oct
Sites: 15
Maximum RV length: No restriction
Facilities: Portable toilets, picnic tables, fire rings
Fee per night: $
Pets: Leashed pets permitted
Activities: Fishing, boating
Management: Wood County Park District
Contact: (419) 353-1897 or (800) 321-1897; www.woodcountyparkdistrict.org. No reservations are taken; all sites are first come, first served.
Finding the campground: From Toledo, follow SR 25 south for 8.8 miles. Turn left to stay on SR 25 and go another 1.1 miles, then turn onto West Boundary Street/SR 25 and go 0.3 mile. Turn right onto West Indiana Avenue/SR 65 and go 2 miles. Turn right onto Hull Prairie Road and go 0.3 mile to the park entrance.
GPS coordinates: N 41 32.849' / W 83 40.288'
Other: There is no drinking water source here. Bring what you need.
About the campground: The "campground" is basically a parking area with a few picnic tables and fire rings. But if you're just looking for a place to hang your hat while you fish, this is it.

A campfire burns in the tent-only camping area on the shores of the Maumee River in Mary Jane Thurston State Park.

Why it's worth a visit: This is the park district's only camping area. It's primitive for sure, but that doesn't keep it from being a favorite of anglers. Its location on the Maumee River makes it a premier spot for those looking to take advantage of the spring walleye migration. This is a pretty good time to look for Maumee River walleyes, too. According to the Ohio Department of Natural Resources, the walleye fishery is in excellent shape, thanks to strong year classes of young fish hatched in 2003, 2007, and 2008. Male walleyes in the 21-inch range and females in the mid-20-inch class should predominate, with smaller fish and some as large as 28 inches mixed in. The minimum size for a fish to be a legal keeper is 15 inches; creel limits vary by season, so check the regulations book that comes with your fishing license. Most anglers fish the river from shore or by wading, but you can put small boats on it. There are launches on Maple Street and in Orleans Park in Perrysburg. White bass and smallmouth bass are popular with fishermen here, too.

120 Mary Jane Thurston State Park

Location: West of Grand Rapids
Season: May–Dec
Sites: 35, some walk-in only
Maximum RV length: 40 feet
Facilities: Vault toilets, picnic tables, fire rings, electricity, water, sanitary dump station, environmental education programs, playground, horseshoe pits, games and sporting equipment available to loan for campers, marina, boat launch
Fee per night: $$$$
Pets: Permitted at all sites
Activities: Boating, hiking, hunting, fishing
Management: Ohio Department of Natural Resources
Contact: (419) 832-7662; www.dnr.state.oh.us/parks/parks/mjthrstn/tabid/768/Default.aspx. For reservations call (866) 644-6727 or visit www.ohio.reserveworld.com.
Finding the campground: From the town of Grand Rapids, head west on West Second Street/SR 65 for a little less than a mile. The entrance to the park will be on the right. If you get to the park office, you've gone too far.
GPS coordinates: N 41 24.596' / W 83 52.672'
Other: Additional walk-in sites of an even more rustic nature are available in the North Turkeyfoot Area of the park. Permits are required and can be obtained at the park office.
About the campground: The main tent camping area is in a nice field. There's a cold shower—a spigot on an upright pipe without any type of enclosure—that allows you to clean up a little bit anyway.
Why it's worth a visit: This area was once part of the Great Black Swamp, a chunk of marshy ground 120 miles long by as much as 40 miles wide that slowed western settlement. Today, Mary Jane Thurston State Park is much more inviting. It offers some excellent waterfowl hunting in the Turkeyfoot Area. The fishing on the Maumee River is fine, some of the best flowing water fishing in the state, in fact. Anglers catch smallmouth bass, white bass, northern pike, channel catfish, crappies, and other species, both from shore and from boats. The park contains a launch as well as dock space. There's also pleasant and easy hiking, some of which takes you past canal remnants that are a big part of the region's history. This is also a neat park at which to combine camping

with a family get-together, given one unique building. The park has an enclosed shelter, heated and wheelchair accessible, that was built by workers of the Civilian Conservation Corps in 1936. It's available to rent.

121 East Harbor State Park

Location: North of Sandusky
Season: Year-round
Sites: 571
Maximum RV length: 40 feet
Facilities: Flush toilets, warm showers, sanitary dump station, water, electricity, picnic tables, fire rings, camp store with free WiFi for campers, boat launch, bike rental, sports equipment available for loan, fish cleaning building, full-service marina, disc golf course, environmental education programs
Fee per night: $$$$
Pets: Permitted at some sites
Activities: Fishing, boating, hiking, swimming, hunting, disc golf
Management: Ohio Department of Natural Resources
Contact: (419) 734-4424 park office, (419) 734-5857 campground office; www.dnr.state.oh.us/parks/parks/eastharbor/tabid/733/Default.aspx. For reservations call (866) 644-6727 or visit www.ohio.reserveworld.com.
Finding the campground: From Sandusky, head west on SR 2 for 9.6 miles before merging onto SR 269 north toward Lakeside/Marblehead for 2.4 miles. Turn right onto SR 269/SR 163, go 0.4 mile, then turn left on SR 269 and continue 1 mile before following the signs to CAMPGROUND.
GPS coordinates: N 41 32.701' / W 82 49.221'
Other: East Harbor also rents two deluxe camper cabins and has two rent-an-RV units. The latter are available for weeklong rental only.
About the campground: This is the largest campground in Ohio's state system and one of the most crowded campgrounds you're ever likely to come across. It's a spit of land between two harbors at Lake Erie, and planners have made use of every inch of ground it offers. Some facilities are limited during the off-season.
Why it's worth a visit: This park is located right on Lake Erie, so of course the main attraction is the Great Lake itself. Lake Erie is known as the "walleye capital of the world" and the fishermen who ply the waters—and their catches—are proof of that. You can also ski, tube, cruise, and more on the lake. There's a marina to cater to everyone's needs as well as a 1,500-foot swimming beach. What is a little surprising is the other opportunities available. There are eleven hiking trails, the longest about 2.5 miles long, that take you along the beach, through the campground and to bird watching platforms from which you can see all kinds of waterfowl. While here, be sure to visit Marblehead Lighthouse State Park. There's no camping, but the lighthouse is the oldest one in continuous use on Lake Erie. It's been in operation since 1822. Tours of it and an accompanying museum are offered weekdays and some weekends throughout summer.

122 Kelleys Island State Park

Location: North of Port Clinton
Season: May–Dec
Sites: 127
Maximum RV length: 50 feet
Facilities: Flush toilets, warm showers, water, sanitary dump station, electricity, picnic tables fire rings, playground, volleyball court, games and sporting equipment available to loan for campers, boat launch, rentals
Fee per night: $$$$
Pets: Permitted at some sites
Activities: Boating, swimming, fishing, hunting
Management: Ohio Department of Natural Resources
Contact: (419) 746-2546 (seasonal); www.dnr.state.oh.us/parks/parks/lakeerie/kelleys/tabid/18980/Default.aspx. For reservations call (866) 644-6727 or visit www.ohio.reserve world.com.
Finding the campground: This park is, as its name suggests, on an island, so you can't drive here directly. But privately operated ferries offer frequent daily service for cars, RVs, bicyclists, and pedestrians from the mainland at Marblehead (www.kelleysislandferry.com) and Sandusky (www .jet-express.com, 800-245-1538). Golf carts and bicycles are available for rent from private vendors. You can also check with the Lake Erie Shores and Island Welcome Center for travel options by visiting www.shoresandislands.com or calling (800) 255-3743.
GPS coordinates: N 41 36.865' / W 82 42.373'
Other: This park has an organized group tenting area, as well as two rent-a-camp sites and two yurts..
About the campground: This is a relatively spacious campground, considering the limited size of the island. Sites 112 to 129 are closest to the swimming beach and changing house.
Why it's worth a visit: Literally located on an island in Lake Erie, Kelleys Island is one of the most interesting parks you may ever find. It's home to a couple of natural features unlike anything else you'll find in Ohio. There are two nature preserves, the North Shore and the North Pond. The former features low cliffs, limestone shelves, and thin soil that, while incapable of growing many trees, does support prairie grasses and rare plants including northern bog violet, lakeside daisy, balsam squaw weed, and Pringle's aster. The latter is a 30-acre marsh and swamp forest. It is one of the few natural, high-quality marshes left in all of the Great Lakes. It's a tremendous place to look for and photograph birds, with literally hundreds of species—including nesting bald eagles—present at any one time. You can also sometimes find here such unusual species as the Lake Erie watersnake and the eastern fox snake, often mistaken for a rattler because of its habit of shaking its tail when alarmed. Be sure to check out the Glacial Grooves, too. A National Natural Landmark, they are marks carved into solid limestone by a slowly creeping glacier 18,000 years ago. The grooves are 400 feet long, 35 feet wide and up to 10 feet deep, with visible marine fossils believed to be 350 to 400 million years old.

123 South Bass Island/Oak Point State Park

Location: North of Port Clinton
Season: May–Dec
Sites: 135
Maximum RV length: 45 feet
Facilities: Flush toilets, warm showers, electricity, water, picnic tables, fire rings, sanitary dump station, boat ramp, playground, shelter house, fish cleaning station
Fee per night: $$$$
Pets: Permitted at some sites
Activities: Boating, swimming, fishing
Management: Ohio Department of Natural Resources
Contact: (419) 285-2112 (seasonally); www.dnr.state.oh.us/parks/parks/lakeerie/sobass/tabid/81/Default.aspx. For reservations call (866) 644-6727 or visit www.ohio.reserveworld.com.
Finding the campground: This is another park that you don't drive to, but access with your own boat or via one of several ferry services. Miller Boat Line offers service for cars, RVS, bicyclists, and pedestrians from the mainland at Catawba; visit www.millerferry.com or call (800) 500-2421. The Jet Express offers service for pedestrians from Port Clinton and Sandusky; visit www.jet-express.com or call (800) 245-1538.
GPS coordinates: N 41 38.765' / W 82 50.310'
Other: This park has an organized group tenting area and rents a rustic cabin as well as four "cabents," which are a combination cabin and tent, with wooden walls, kitchen, TV, and more, all under a canvas roof.
About the campground: At South Bass, sites 95 to 101 and 112 to 117 are closest to the water, while 130 to 135 are closest to the beach and playground.
Why it's worth a visit: South Bass Island/Oak Point is actually two separate tracts of land on the same island, each with its own name, but so close as to be essentially one facility. South Bass is on the island's western edge, as is the campground. It's also the larger of the two parks, even at a mere 33 acres (the whole island is only 3.7 miles wide by 1.5 miles long). The park is a scenic landmark when viewed from the water and in turn offers great views of the lake from its shores. The wooded campground and lakeside picnic area are a quiet retreat, especially compared to nearby Put-In-Bay. Sometimes called "the Key West of Lake Erie," it's located on the island's eastern side. If you do head into Put-In-Bay, visit Perry's Victory and International Peace Monument. It pays tribute to Oliver Hazard Perry, who won control of Lake Erie for American forces in the War of 1812. The site is a national park that offers tours of the 352-foot monument and lighthouse. Oak Point, meanwhile, is closer to the island's northern edge. It offers facilities for boaters, including docks where you can put your boat overnight. There are also opportunities to picnic close to the heart of town.

124 Middle Bass Island State Park

Location: North of Port Clinton
Season: Mid-May–Oct
Sites: 21, for tents only
Maximum RV length: N/A
Facilities: Vault toilets, picnic tables, fire rings, marina, miniature golf course
Fee per night: $$$
Pets: Leashed pets permitted
Activities: Boating, fishing, golfing, biking
Management: Ohio Department of Natural Resources
Contact: (412) 285-0311 (seasonally); www.dnr.state.oh.us/parks/parks/middlebass/
tabid/766/Default.aspx. For reservations call (866) 644-6727 or visit www.ohio.reserve
world.com.
Finding the campground: There is no vehicle access to this park, but there are shuttle services
available from Port Clinton and Catawba Bay.
GPS coordinates: N 41 40.555' / W 82 48.716'
Other: You're not permitted to take alcoholic beverages off your boat here, so if you bring it, be
sure to keep it on your craft.
About the campground: There is no drinking water available at this campground, so be prepared
to bring your own or to get it from the marina. The marina also has showers and flush toilets. There
was, at the time of this writing, no map of the campground.
Why it's worth a visit: This island is not comprised solely of the state park. There's a whole town
here, with a fire station, cemetery, post office, ball fields, even an airport. Exploring the town is
interesting stuff, either by walking or bicycling. The park and its marina are on the island's south-
ern end. That marina is what you need to pay attention to most. It's where you will find most of the
services you need, some of them in a newly opened harbormaster building that includes a laun-
dry, gift and snack shops, and additional showers. There's some natural history worth looking for,
too. The island is home to Ohio's densest concentration of fox snakes, a harmless but interesting
reptile, as well as water snakes. You'll also find impressive stands of red cedar and some caverns.

125 White Star Park

Location: West of Fremont
Season: Apr–mid-Nov
Sites: 48
Maximum RV length: 45 feet for most sites, 88 feet for the two pull-through sites
Facilities: Vault toilets, water, electricity, sanitary dump station, picnic tables, fire rings, play-
ground, volleyball court, boat launch
Fee per night: $$$ to $$$$
Pets: Leashed pets permitted
Activities: Hiking, fishing, boating, swimming, scuba diving, hunting, horseback riding, biking,
geocaching

A scuba diver adjusts his equipment after surfacing in the old quarry lake at White Star Park.

Management: Sandusky County Park District
Contact: (419) 334-4495; www.lovemyparks.com/parks/white_star_park. No reservations are taken; it's first come, first served.
Finding the campground: From Fremont, head west on Hayes Avenue/US 6 for 10.6 miles. Turn right onto SR 300 and go 2.2 miles. The entrance to the campground will be on the left.
GPS coordinates: N 41 22.414' / W 83 19.226'
Other: This is one of two parks in Sandusky County open to hunting. You need to secure a permit, though. They're available by calling (419) 355-7066.
About the campground: The sites here—twenty-four modern, twenty-four rustic—are in the open, with some on the edge of the woods and others centered in a field. Organized youth groups can camp for free with two weeks notice.
Why it's worth a visit: This 797-acre park is an interesting one, to be sure. Like many parks, it has a lake that serves as the center of much activity. That means swimming, boating, and fishing for species such as bluegills, bullhead and channel catfish, trout, bass, and yellow perch. Here, though, the lake is also a haven for scuba divers. This was an old limestone quarry and the water is exceptionally clear, so much so that this is considered one of the finest inland diving locations in Ohio. There are some underwater "trails," too. They allow divers to explore a sunken police cruiser, motorcycle, boats, and a panel truck. There are also a couple of crusher holes, statues of seahorses, a concrete Pandora figure, a block house, and an "enchanted forest." A small dive shop operated on weekends can supply you with rental gear and oxygen. There is a fee to dive, and no solitary diving is allowed for safety reasons, but night diving is on Sat nights between Memorial Day and the end of Sept. For information call White Star Quarry at (419) 637-3483 or visit www.whitestarquarry.com.

126 Wolf Creek Park

Location: South of Fremont
Season: Apr–mid-Nov
Sites: 24
Maximum RV length: 45 feet
Facilities: Vault toilets, water, picnic tables, fire rings, playground
Fee per night: $$$
Pets: Leashed pets permitted
Activities: Hiking, biking, fishing, paddling
Management: Sandusky County Park District
Contact: (419) 334-4495; www.lovemyparks.com/parks/wolf_creek_park. No reservations are taken; it's first come, first served with self-registration.
Finding the campground: From Fremont, follow Hayes Avenue west for 2.6 miles. Turn left onto SR 53 south and go 6 miles to the campground.
GPS coordinates: N 41 16.521' / W 83 10.086'
Other: Organized youth groups can camp for free with two weeks notice.
About the campground: Registration is done on the honor system. A kiosk at the campground entrance is available for deposits.
Why it's worth a visit: Relatively tiny at just 93 acres, Wolf Creek Park is nonetheless a place where you can have fun. It's located along the Sandusky River so there's access to canoeing, kayaking, and fishing. The Sandusky has been a state-designated scenic river since 1970. It flows through some of the richest farmland in the Midwest and is generally smooth and easy to float. It's striking, too. Exposed limestone outcroppings mark its route, and the annual runs of walleyes and white bass make it a favorite of anglers. There's some history to see along the river. The Mull Covered Bridge was built in 1851 and remained in service until 1962. Today, on the National Register of Historic Places and maintained by the county, it's an interesting piece of Ohio's past. There's also hiking available, with two loop trails, one about a mile and the other a third of a mile. A part of the 1,400-plus mile Buckeye Trail passes through the park as well.

Central

Central Ohio is the smallest of the five regions and the one with the fewest parks offering camping. But it's not to be overlooked.

It is, more than anything, a place to visit if you like to spend your time on the water. There are lakes for every taste. Alum Creek State Park offers the whopper of them all, a lake that encompasses almost 3,400 acres. It's home to the largest inland beach in Ohio. Deer Creek State Park has a 1,300-acre lake of its own, as does Delaware State Park. All allow opportunities to run and gun on the water with skis and tubes.

If you want to travel a bit slower, North Branch Kokosing River Lake limits boats to 10 horsepower. The lakes in Mt. Gilead and A.W. Marion State Parks are open only to boats with electric motors and unpowered craft. They're perfect for fishing and cruising.

The hidden gem of the region is Pastime Park. Run by the Village of Plain City, it's a small community park. Lots of groups come here to stay and play. But it's ideal for camping, too. The large swimming pool with its slides and other attractions are perfect for kids.

Away from the parks, the region has some equally fun places to visit. How about a popcorn museum? The Wyandot Popcorn Museum bills itself as being home to the world's largest collection of popcorn poppers and peanut roasters. And chocolate? The area is home to a factory that makes that, too. The Schakolad Chocolate Factory offers field trips and chocolate-making camps. The North Market, very near the Columbus Convention Center, is a giant open-air market perfect for an afternoon stroll. You can find products from local farmers. There are cooking classes, microbrew festivals, artisan events, and more, so if you want to sample some local fare or learn to use those ingredients to make your own creations, this is the place for that.

For a small region, there are lots of opportunities. Pick a starting point and get rolling.

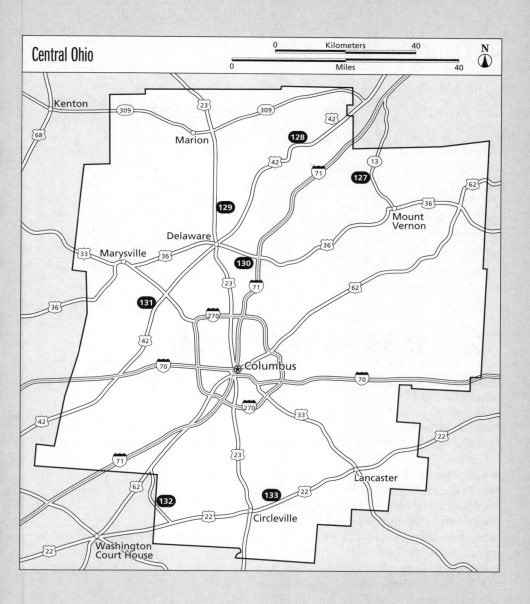

Central Ohio

Kilometers
0   40

Miles
0   40

N

Kenton

309

68

23

309

42

Marion

128

42

129

71

13

127

62

36

Mount
Vernon

Delaware

36

Marysville

33

36

130

23

71

62

131

42

36

270

70

Columbus

70

42

270

33

22

71

23

Lancaster

62

132

133

22

22

Circleville

22

Washington
Court House

The Center of It All

	total sites	hookups	max RV lengths	toilets	showers	drinking water	dump station	recreation	fee	reservation
127 North Branch Kokosing River Lake	100	Y	50	F	Y	Y	Y	HBFCLU	$$$$	Y
128 Mt. Gilead State Park	59	Y	50	V	N	Y	Y	HFBLREE	$$$$	Y
129 Delaware State Park	211	Y	50	F	Y	Y	Y	HFBSLUEE	$$$$	Y
130 Alum Creek State Park	286	Y	50	F	Y	Y	Y	HBFSCLRUEE	$$$$	Y
131 Pastime Park	50	Y	N/A	F	Y	Y	Y	HS	$$$-$$$$	N
132 Deer Creek State Park	227	Y	50	F	Y	Y	Y	HBFSCLRUEE	$$$$	Y
133 A.W. Marion State Park	58	Y	50	V	N	Y	Y	HBFSL	$$$$	Y

See fee codes on page xx and amenities codes on page xxiii.

127 North Branch Kokosing River Lake

Location: North of Fredericktown
Season: Apr 1–Oct 31
Sites: 100
Maximum RV length: 50 feet
Facilities: Flush toilets, showers, electricity, water, sanitary dump station, picnic tables, fire rings, boat ramps
Fee per night: $$$$
Pets: Leashed pets permitted
Activities: Fishing, boating, hiking, biking, hunting
Management: Muskingum Watershed Conservancy District
Contact: For reservations call (740) 694-1900; http://corpslakes.usace.army.mil/visitors/projects.cfm?Id=H112690.
Finding the campground: From Fredericktown, follow Waterford Road/County Road 6 west to the park entrance, then follow signs to CAMPGROUND.
GPS coordinates: N 40 30.371' / W 82 35.191'
Other: This campground was formerly operated by the US Army Corps of Engineers. The lake still is.
About the campground: This campground is located on the waterfront, so it's a very pretty one.
Why it's worth a visit: North Branch Kokosing River Lake is tiny by US Army Corps of Engineers standards at just 154 acres. Its small size and 10-horsepower limit makes it a quiet and peaceful place to relax. The fishing can be good, though the northern end of the lake is somewhat silted in. It's not overly deep anywhere. But there are channel catfish, bass, and panfish available. There's some good and varied hunting here, too. The area around the northern end of the lake contains a lot of fields, fencerows, and field dividers, so look for ring-necked pheasants and rabbits there.

Rabbits are also pretty common along stream bottoms and marsh areas. The southern end of the lake contains a lot of pin oaks and hickories and so is home to fox and gray squirrels and deer. Two gravel travel lanes allow those in wheelchairs to enter the wildlife area, either to hunt or to observe wildlife.

128 Mt. Gilead State Park

Location: East of Mt. Gilead
Season: May–Dec
Sites: 59
Maximum RV length: 50 feet
Facilities: Vault toilets, electricity, waste-water drains, water, picnic tables, fire rings, camp store, playground, games and sporting equipment available to loan for campers, environmental education programs, launch ramp
Fee per night: $$$$
Pets: Permitted at some sites
Activities: Fishing on two lakes, boating with electric motors only, hiking, horseback riding
Management: Ohio Department of Natural Resources
Contact: (419) 946-1961, seasonally, (740) 548-4631 care of Alum Creek State Park otherwise; www.dnr.state.oh.us/parks/parks/mtgilead/tabid/772/Default.aspx. For reservations call (866) 644-6727 or visit www.ohio.reserveworld.com. Some sites are first come, first served.
Finding the campground: From Mt. Gilead, head east on SR 95 for about 1 mile. Turn left into the MAIN CAMPGROUND at the signs.
GPS coordinates: N 40 32.872' / W 82 48.624'
Other: This park also rents two deluxe camper cabins and has an organized group tenting area. Campsite reservations are local sale only in Nov and Dec.
About the campground: This campground is two arms with circular loops on their ends. The sites on the loops offer the most space and most privacy, though one is also the location of the park's two cabins. A hiking trail that follows the edge of the campground leads to the nature center and lake.
Why it's worth a visit: Mt. Gilead is one of the smallest parks in the state system, at least when it comes to those that offer overnight facilities. It's just 181 acres. That sets the scene for relaxed, quiet camping. There are two lakes, one built in 1919, the other in 1930, where you can fish for bass and bluegills. The larger of the two, 32-acre Mt. Gilead Lake, is also open to paddlers, so there are opportunities to cruise around with your fishing rod or camera, looking for waterbirds and mammals like muskrats. There are seven combination hiking and equestrian trails, with the one that parallels Whetstone Creek especially easy and interesting if you've got kids who like to look for crayfish and salamanders. Don't miss an opportunity to explore the nearby town of Marion while in the area. Only about a mile from the park, it's where you'll find a museum based in what was President Warren G. Harding's home. Tours are offered seasonally.

Yellow daylilies, still wet with rain, mark the entrance to the campground at Delaware State Park.

129 Delaware State Park

Location: South of Marion
Season: Apr–Dec
Sites: 211, some ADA accessible
Maximum RV length: 50 feet
Facilities: Flush toilets, warm showers, sanitary dump station, electricity, water, picnic tables, fire rings, laundry facilities, volleyball, basketball and tetherball courts, horseshoe pits, playground, bike rental, games and sporting equipment available to loan for campers, marina, boat launch, environmental education programs
Fee per night: $$$$
Pets: Permitted at some sites
Activities: Hiking, boating with unlimited horsepower, fishing, swimming, disc golf, hunting
Management: Ohio Department of Natural Resources
Contact: (740) 363-4561 campground, seasonally, (740) 548-4631 care of Alum Creek State Park otherwise; www.dnr.state.oh.us/parks/parks/delaware/tabid/729/Default.aspx. For reservations call (866) 644-6727 or visit www.ohio.reserveworld.com. There are also some first come, first served sites.
Finding the campground: From Marion, head south on Marion-Waldo Road/SR 423 for 5.8 miles. Turn left onto East Bethlehem Road, go 0.6 mile, then take the first right onto US 23 south for 7.4 miles and follow the signs to CAMPGROUND.
GPS coordinates: N 40 22.672' / W 83 04.416'
Other: This park also rents three yurts and has an organized group tenting area.
About the campground: This campground is composed of four loops, with campsites branching off the center hub like the petals on a flower. All of the sites are fairly close together, but also near the lake and hiking. Sites are local sale only from Oct–Mar.
Why it's worth a visit: Yet another US Army Corps of Engineers facility run by the state as a park, Delaware contains a 1,300-acre lake. The southern half of it, from camp area 3 south, is open to unlimited horsepower boating; the northern half is a no-wake zone. You can swim in the lake, at either its public beach or one of its two boat-swim areas. There are fish to be caught, too. But if you want to try something a little different, visit Delaware Wildlife Area, which is on the park's eastern side. It's home to more than fifty ponds that hold populations of bass, bluegills, catfish, and crappies. The area is also popular with hunters who chase rabbits, pheasants, doves, and deer and at other times use the handgun, rifle, shotgun, and archery ranges. Birders should make a point of exploring this area, too. In addition to holding the usual songbirds and waterfowl, it's home to all manner of raptors. You'll see the greatest variety during their fall migration, but all summer long the area is home to red-tailed hawks, American kestrels, and northern harriers.

A young Forster's tern that was diving for fish soars over the water at Alum Creek State Park.

130 Alum Creek State Park

Location: Southeast of Cheshire
Season: Mid-Apr–Dec
Sites: 286
Maximum RV length: 50 feet
Facilities: Flush toilets, warm showers, sanitary dump station, electricity, water, picnic tables, fire rings, boat launch, basketball courts, horseshoe pits, playgrounds, camp store with free WiFi, environmental education programs, dog park, boat launch
Fee per night: $$$$
Pets: Permitted on some sites
Activities: Hiking, mountain biking, horseback riding, fishing, disc golf, hunting, swimming, unlimited horsepower boating
Management: Ohio Department of Natural Resources
Contact: www.dnr.state.oh.us/parks/parks/alum/tabid/711/Default.aspx. For reservations call (740) 548-4039 or (740) 548-4631 or visit www.ohio.reserveworld.com.
Finding the campground: From Delaware, head south on US 23 for 2.8 miles. Turn left onto Cheshire Road, go 0.5 mile, then turn right onto Braumiller Road and go 0.04 mile. Turn left on Cheshire Road and go 2.9 miles, then go right onto South Old State Road for 0.2 mile to the campground.
GPS coordinates: N 40 14.231' / W 82 59.219'

Other: This park also has an equestrian camp with thirty primitive sites and four camper cabins, one extra-large cabin and three cedar cabins. Boaters can also stay overnight on their craft in the Sailing Association and 36/37 coves.

About the campground: This is another large, crowded campground. The sites vary tremendously: some are in sun, some in shade, some overlooking the lake. All have electricity, but some facilities are limited in the off-season.

Why it's worth a visit: This is a 3,387-acre US Army Corps of Engineers lake run as a state park, and it has the requisite Army Corps visitor center, so you'll want to check that out. But there's a lot to do outside. Alum Creek is home to the largest inland beach in the state park system—a 3,000 foot expanse—though campers have exclusive access to their own beach and boat launch, too. You can boat and hunt here, but in both cases, the park can be split into halves. North of Cheshire Road offers the best hunting for squirrels and deer, as well as quieter boating with tree-lined shores, sheltered inlets, and shale cliffs that result from water cutting through bedrock. South of Cheshire Road you can find good hunting for rabbits and upland birds, as well as unlimited horsepower boating. That's why skiers and tubers congregate here. And if you want to bike, hike, or ride your horse, the park takes in 4,630 acres of woods and fields. Mountain bikers will find three trails—one each for beginner, intermediate, and advanced riders—while equestrians have 38 miles to call their own.

131   Pastime Park

Location: West of Dublin
Season: Apr 1–Oct 31
Sites: 50 plus
Maximum RV length: No restriction
Facilities: Showers, flush toilets, electricity, water, sanitary dump station nearby, picnic tables, playground, disc golf course, baseball fields, horseshoe courts, basketball courts
Fee per night: $$$ to $$$$
Pets: Leashed pets permitted
Activities: Hiking, geocaching, swimming, sports
Management: Village of Plain City
Contact: (614) 873-3527; www.plain-city.com/parks/pastime-park. Reservations are required only of groups of 20 or more; otherwise, it's first come, first served.
Finding the campground: From Dublin, follow US 33 west for 3 miles. Take the SR 161/Post Road exit toward Plain City, go 0.2 mile, then turn left to stay on SR 161 and go another 0.4 mile. Take the second left at the next roundabout to stay on SR 161 and go another 4.4 miles. Turn right onto North Chillicothe Street and go 0.5 mile. The entrance to the park and campground will be on the left.
GPS coordinates: N 40 06.893' / W 83 16.227'
Other: No alcoholic beverages are permitted.
About the campground: When entering the campground from North Chilicothe Street, you'll pass the camp office and self-registration station.
Why it's worth a visit: This park is a scenic one, with oak trees one-hundred years old and older throughout the area. Two things make it stand out. The first is its brand-new Aquatic Center.

It's a giant swim center with a "zero depth" and spray area for the smallest of children, a water slide and diving board for older swimmers, and fitness classes and designated swim times for seniors. Lessons are available, too. The second is the full schedule of events hosted at the park throughout the year. There's a "music in the park" series of concerts each June–Aug, the Miami Valley Steam Threshers Show and Mid-Ohio Classic Scooters Show. The latter features classic motorcycles and scooters.

132 Deer Creek State Park

Location: South of Mt. Sterling
Season: Year-round
Sites: 227, some walk-in only
Maximum RV length: 50 feet
Facilities: Flush toilets, warm showers, sanitary dump station, electricity, picnic tables, fire rings, water, playgrounds, miniature golf, basketball, volleyball and tetherball courts, horseshoe pits, bike rentals, marina, boat launch, nature center, environmental education programs
Fee per night: $$$$
Pets: Permitted on some sites
Activities: Boating with unlimited horsepower, fishing, swimming, hiking, mountain biking, horseback riding, golf, hunting
Management: Ohio Department of Natural Resources
Contact: (740) 869-3124 park office, (740) 869-3508 campground, seasonally; www.dnr.state .oh.us/parks/parks/deercrk/tabid/725/Default.aspx. For reservations call (866) 644-6727 or visit www.ohio.reserveworld.com.
Finding the campground: From Mt. Sterling, follow SR 207 south for 3.8 miles. Turn left onto Dawson-Yankeetown Road and go 1.5 miles, then turn right onto Waterloo Road and follow the signs.
GPS coordinates: N 39 38.567' / W 83 14.785'
Other: This park also has twenty-five cottages, two camper cabins, a 110-room lodge and conference center, a group camp and a primitive equestrian camp. There's also a rent-a-camp site where you get a tent on a platform, a light, cook stove, and more so that you can camp without bringing all of your own equipment.
About the campground: All sites are rented on a local sale-only basis, meaning through the park directly, from Jan–Mar, when facilities are limited.
Why it's worth a visit: Deer Creek State park is popular with vacationers because of all that it offers. Boaters can cruise or zip around 1,277-acre Cree Creek Lake, a US Army Corps impoundment that places no limits on horsepower. Fishermen can chase bass, walleyes, muskies, and panfish or its famous concentrations of saugeyes, which congregate in the spillway below the dam each spring. There's a full-service marina catering to all those users. The park also has a 1,700-foot swimming beach and an 18-hole golf course that features ten ponds and fifty-two sand traps. There are hiking, biking and equestrian trails to be explored, with several originating in or adjacent to the campground. You can also use Deer Creek as the launching pad for visiting nearby attractions. Deer Creek Wildlife Area is managed for upland game hunting, so if you've got a bird dog, it's a great place to try. If you prefer history, you could visit Adena State Memorial, home to Ohio's first US Senator and the state's

Canada geese are a common sight at A.W. Marion State Park.

only plantation-style complex, or Sugarloaf Mountain Amphitheater, which depicts the life story of Tecumseh, the legendary Native American leader, on outdoor stages.

133 A.W. Marion State Park

Location: West of New Strasburg
Season: Apr–Oct
Sites: 58, some walk-in only
Maximum RV length: 50 feet
Facilities: Vault toilets, water, electricity, sanitary dump station, picnic tables, fire rings, boat rentals, boat launch, playground, games and sporting equipment available to loan for campers, volleyball and basketball courts, horseshoe pits
Fee per night: $$$$
Pets: Leashed pets permitted
Activities: Fishing, hiking, swimming off boats in a designated area, hunting, boating with electric motors only
Management: Ohio Department of Natural Resources
Contact: (740) 869-3124, care of Deer Creek State Park; www.dnr.state.oh.us/parks/parks/awmarion/tabid/712/Default.aspx. For reservations call (866) 644-6727 or visit www.ohio.reserveworld.com.

Finding the campground: From New Strasburg, head west on US 22 for about 5 miles. Turn right onto TH 42/Ringgold Southern Road and follow it until you can turn left onto Warner-Huffner Road.
GPS coordinates: N 39 38.071' / W 82 52.527'
Other: This park has a site for organized group camping.
About the campground: This small campground consists of three loops. The walk-in sites offer nice privacy, as do sites 51 and 52, though the latter are closest to the playground.
Why it's worth a visit: This is a relatively tiny park, encompassing just 309 acres, but that makes it perfect if your idea of camping is to go where things are quiet, relaxed, and peaceful. You can experience that here. There are opportunities to boat and fish on A.W. Marion's 145-acre Hargus Lake, but only unpowered craft and those with electric motors are permitted, so you don't have to worry about being buzzed by jet-powered motorboats. You can swim, too, but only in designated areas from your boat; there is no beach. There's hiking on two trails, one of which encircles the lake, and all of it pretty easy walking. Venture outside the park and within easy driving distance are two state-run nature preserves, Stage's Pond and Shallenberger Preserve. The former is home to waterfowl, herons, shorebirds, and all kinds of life associated with wetlands; the latter is famous for its unique plants, such as mountain laurel, which is rare this far west of the Appalachian Mountains.

Appendix: Packing list

Who hasn't been there? You leave home, drive a considerable distance to your camp-site, then realize you've left some essential piece of equipment at home. It might be your raincoat or your camp axe or a lighter for the stove and lanterns. Whatever it is, it's something you need and can't get readily.

To avoid that kind of frustration, print a copy of the following and keep it in your camping bin or tote. You might want more than is listed here or less, depending on how you travel. But whenever you are planning to leave home, pull it out and check off items as you pack them in your vehicle. That won't necessarily guarantee you'll always have everything you need on hand, but it helps.

Your list should include:

❒ Reservation paperwork. If you called ahead or reserved space online, take your receipt or confirmation with you.

❒ Backpack, daypack, and/or fanny pack

❒ Bags (grocery bags, always handy for holding odds and ends)

❒ Ice chest with ice

❒ Lantern (with propane, liquid fuel, or batteries, as appropriate, and some extra mantles)

❒ Flashlights or headlamps, with batteries and spare bulbs

❒ Matches, preferably waterproof, and/or a lighter

❒ Tent

❒ Tent rain tarp

❒ Extra tent stakes

❒ Dining fly

❒ Plastic ground cloth for under the tent

❒ Sleeping bag

❒ Sleeping mattress or pad (along with a method of inflating it)

❒ Pillow

❒ Space blanket

❒ Sunscreen

❒ Insect repellent

❒ Poison ivy block

❒ Poison ivy remedies

❒ Allergy medicines

❒ Pain relief pills, like aspirin or acetaminophen

❒ Stomach medicines (for diarrhea, upset stomach, etc.)

❏ Tweezers for splinters

❏ Antiseptic

❏ Band–Aids and bandages

❏ Itch cream for bug bites

❏ Mole skin to prevent blisters if you hike a lot

❏ A first–aid kit that you can take with you on a hike or canoe trip

❏ Prescription medicines

❏ Extra glasses or contact lenses, and a glasses–repair kit

❏ Biodegradable soap

❏ Washcloth

❏ Bath towel

❏ Biodegradable shampoo

❏ Biodegradable toothpaste

❏ Toothbrush

❏ Comb or hair brush

❏ Razor and shaving cream

❏ Toilet paper (the stuff in state park campgrounds is notoriously cheap, earning more complaints from visitors than just about anything else)

❏ A case or bag for carrying everything to the shower house

❏ Bathing suit

❏ Water shoes

❏ Extra dry shoes

❏ Sunglasses

❏ Axe

❏ Bow saw

❏ Extension cord for campsites with an electric hookup

❏ Duct tape and/or electrical tape

❏ Hammer for pounding in tent pegs

❏ Rope

❏ Clothesline

❏ Clothespins

❏ Whiskbroom to clean table and tent site

❏ Pocket knife

❏ Compass and area map

❏ Fishing pole, gear, license, and lures or bait

❏ Beach chairs

- ❏ Camping chairs
- ❏ Safety pins
- ❏ Cell phone with your car adapter
- ❏ Camera with good batteries
- ❏ Camcorder, also with good batteries
- ❏ Money, credit card, and ID (needed to get your senior discount, if nothing else)
- ❏ Books, radio, cards, games, toys, etc.
- ❏ Sports equipment
- ❏ Citronella candles
- ❏ Binoculars
- ❏ Field guides for identifying wildlife
- ❏ Clothing appropriate for the season. Remember, though, that it never hurts to have extra dry socks and an extra sweatshirt or jacket in case the nights get cooler than expected.
- ❏ Wide-brimmed hat to block the sun
- ❏ Jacket
- ❏ Rain gear or poncho (which can double as an emergency lean-to if you're on the trail)
- ❏ Shower shoes
- ❏ Hiking boots
- ❏ Hiking staff
- ❏ Work gloves
- ❏ A few simple tools (hammer, pliers, tape, screwdrivers)
- ❏ Stove with fuel and lighter or charcoal and lighter fluid and grill
- ❏ Newspapers or some other tinder for lighting a campfire
- ❏ Firewood
- ❏ Frying pan with lid
- ❏ Cooking skewers for hot dogs, marshmallows, etc.
- ❏ Pot or sauce pan with lid
- ❏ Can opener
- ❏ Tongs
- ❏ Coffeemaker and filters
- ❏ Pot lifter and/or pot holders
- ❏ Tablecloth
- ❏ Plates
- ❏ Mugs/cups
- ❏ Knives, forks, spoons

- ❏ Kitchen knife
- ❏ Mixing bowl
- ❏ Spatula
- ❏ Scrub pad
- ❏ Dish pan for washing dishes
- ❏ Container for water
- ❏ Paper towels and napkins
- ❏ Trash bags
- ❏ Plastic Bags
- ❏ Aluminum foil
- ❏ Biodegradable dish soap
- ❏ Water bottle to carry while hiking
- ❏ Water jug to fetch water from the pump or faucet
- ❏ Food and drinks, remembering that you'll have only as much capacity to keep things cold as you have cooler space. You—and your children especially—will be sure to work up hearty appetites being outdoors all day, though, so pack a good amount of food, including any condiments/spices you like for cooking. Fresh fruit and vegetables are always good options as they are quick and need no refrigeration, as are things like granola bars and trail mix.
- ❏ Hunting gear appropriate for the game you will be pursuing
- ❏ Dog food if you're bringing a pet
- ❏ Dog leash

Index

Timbre Ridge Lake, 74
Tuscarawas County
  Fairgrounds, 25
Twin Creek
  MetroPark, 108

V
Van Buren State
  Park, 125
Van Wert County
  Fairgrounds, 122
Vesuvius Horse Trail, 75

Vinton Furnace State
  Experimental Forest
  Hunting Camp, 64

W
Washington County
  Fairgrounds, 60
West Branch State
  Park, 14
White Star Park, 135
Wildcat Hollow Hiking
  Trail, 49

Williams County
  Fairgrounds, 125
Winton Woods
  Campground, 95
Wolf Creek Park, 137
Wolf Run State Park, 47

Z
Zaleski State Forest
  Horse Camp, 63

About the Author

Bob Frye is the outdoors editor for the *Tribune-Review* newspaper in Pittsburgh, Pennsylvania. He is the author of numerous other books, including *Best Hikes Near Pittsburgh, Best Easy Day Hikes: Pittsburgh, Paddling Pennsylvania, Camping Pennsylvania* and *Deer Wars: Science, Tradition and the Battle Over Managing Whitetails in Pennsylvania*. He lives in North Huntingdon with his wife, Amanda, sons, Derek and Tyler, and springer spaniel Remi.

Your next adventure begins here.

falcon.com